Getting
GooseBumps

Second Edition

A pragmatic guide to effective inbound marketing

Emotionally connect with your audience
and achieve your business objectives

Written by Bryan Adams and Dave Hazlehurst
Illustrated by Daniel Schooler

Ph.Creative

www.ph-creative.com

Second edition published in March 2018 by:

Wordscapes Ltd.
Northern Lights Building
5 Mann Street
Liverpool L8 5AF
www.wordscape.org.uk

First published in 2015 by Wordscapes Ltd.

ISBN: 978-0-9955594-9-3

A CIP Catalogue record for this book is available from the British Library.

Written by Bryan Adams and Dave Hazlehurst
Editors: Emma-Lee Curtis and Kathryn Lamble
Design, typesetting and production: Daniel Schooler
Publisher: Fiona Shaw
Printed in the UK by Buxton Press

"This book presents the in
day storytelling to market
customer in a context that
person to ignore."

portance of modern
g for the love of your
hard for any business

Contents

Chapter 1   31

Getting your story straight
Why it's important to you and your customers and how to ensure you're being authentic.
- The power of getting it right
- The science behind the approach
- The consequence of getting it wrong
- Recommended reading and resources

Chapter 2   45

The right direction
How to align your business objectives with your marketing goals to ensure everyone
in the business is on the same page.
- Writing your digital strategy
- Examples of a digital strategy at work
- Considering your digital tactics
- Defining your objectives
- Examples of digital tactics at work
- Recommended reading and resources

Chapter 3   61

Audiences and the art of listening
How to listen to your audiences' wants, needs and desires in order to maximise your chances of engaging and selling to them.
- Understanding pathos, ethos and logos
- Buyer personas
- Persona mapping and validation
- Recommended reading and resources

Chapter 4   83

Right place, right time
An in depth look at where, when and what your audience spends their time looking at and who they are already influenced by.
- Optimising your content to be found online
- Google updates
- SEO and audience personas
- See. Think. Do. Delight
- Social media and audience personas
- Recommended reading and resources

Chapter 5   103

How to tell a story
Master your ability to effectively communicate with impact and emotional intelligence in order to elicit the desired action.
- The science and art of storytelling for your marketing
- Storytelling – learning from Hollywood
- Storytelling – learning from great leaders
- Storytelling – learning from comedians
- Candidate Experience – a unique model
- Recommended reading and resources

Chapter 6   143

The story so far
How all of the previous components and ideas fit together into one neat plan you can work from and rely on.
- Get the most out of your inbound marketing
- Recommended reading and resources

Acknowledgements

This is the point in the book where we get to extend our thanks to the team at Ph.Creative – they bring the advice contained within this book to life on a daily basis. So, thank you to:

Mike Hazlehurst, Paul Mason, Stevie Crane, Robert Watts, Jenny Middleton, Stewart Bennett, Daniel Trotter, Jake Pittman, Elizabeth McCarthy, Terry Banks, Samantha Hindley, Craig Graham, Alison Miller, Daniel Reese, David Lancaster, George Ellis, Lynne Gregory, Jenni Fleet, Sam Davis, Mike Ng, James Taylor, Heather Duvall, Luke Power, Michael Bowen, Anthony Whitelaw, Dan Booth, Michelle Riches, Mark Russel, Andy Flatman, Helen Adams, Nikki Mistry and Tracey West.

Special acknowledgements

Thanks must go to Jennie Mandelkow for her copy editing and scheduling, keeping us consistently on target.

Thank you to Dan Schooler for creating a beautifully designed and illustrated book.

And last, but by no means least, a special thanks goes to Emma-Lee Curtis and Kathryn Lamble for making sense of it all and for six months of incredible hustle.

We wrote a book, guys!

Get to know the authors

 BRYAN ADAMS

CEO and Founder of digital marketing and employer brand agency, Ph.Creative, Bryan has over 15 years' experience in the field of digital marketing. Regarded by many as one of the UK's key figures in social media and digital marketing he features regularly in top influencer and marketing blogger lists. Bryan is also an accomplished keynote speaker and has spoken at events all over the world, from Thailand to Brazil, the US and throughout Europe.

7 quick-fire questions for Bryan

CAREER HIGH?

Securing £500k investment into the agency. Getting the business 'investment ready' and then being able to invest in excellence has been a real turning point.

CAREER LOW?

There were a few consecutive months in 2005 where I wasn't sure where the money to pay wages would come from. I can't remember where it did come from, but it was tough and very stressful.

BIGGEST ACHIEVEMENT?

I used to have a debilitating fear of public speaking. To overcome the fear I enrolled on a stand-up comedy course and graduated by performing my own material to a crowd of 300 strangers at a comedy festival.

PROUDEST MOMENT?

The birth of my son, Harrison. No question, no competition.

SCARIEST SITUATION?

Jumping out of a plane to conquer a fear of heights did test my resolve, however, it didn't work – I still hate heights and strongly recommend not peeing in a jumpsuit at 30,000ft.

FUNNIEST TALE?

I once cut my head very, very badly (later resulting in a sizeable scar just above my hairline) in a badly lit street in London. As my head bled profusely, I ran around panicking and everybody just ignored or laughed at my antics...It was Halloween. Very funny now, but ironically scary at the time.

MOST EMBARRASSING STORY?

Two minutes before presenting a huge business deal to a small audience, (including NASA, NATO, NY Times and Goldman Sachs) I bent down and shredded the backside of my trousers. I don't know why, but that day was a 'no underwear' day. #PeachGate

DAVE HAZLEHURST

Partner and Director of Client Services at Ph.Creative, Dave brings his relentless energy and passion for all things digital to the agency. Frequently sharing his extensive knowledge as a keynote speaker and workshop leader around the world, Dave has spoken at events for organisations including Google, LinkedIn and The Chartered Institute of Marketing.

7 quick-fire questions for Dave

BIGGEST ACHIEVEMENT?

Being asked by Google to deliver Google expertise to their audience via a Hangout On Air, live from their London base. When the red light turned green I had to talk to a large empty room for 45 minutes. Very strange.

PROUDEST MOMENT?

The birth of my two children, Louie (aka Google Junior) and Ellie.

SCARIEST MOMENT?

Easily, watching the 2005 Champions League final between Liverpool and Milan. At full time the score was 3-3 so we went to penalties. I'm a big Red and the tension got so high I had to hide behind the sofa during the shoot-out.

FUNNIEST TALE?

When I was a kid, my neighbours owned a wooden rocking horse which I absolutely loved. I'd visit their house all the time just to have a go on it! At about midnight one night, I snuck out of my house and actually let myself into theirs! Hearing creaking noises, my neighbours crept downstairs, thinking someone had broken in. Instead, they found me, sitting merrily on their rocking horse, having a whale of a time...

BRAVEST FEAT?

Asking my father-in-law if I could marry my wife, Alison, had me pretty anxious and I don't often get nervous. We were watching a Liverpool match together and the whole time I was running over the scenario in my mind. All of a sudden, Hyypiä scored from a corner – the adrenaline of celebrating just led me to blurting it out, to which he calmly replied 'I'm sure she'd be delighted!'

MOST EMBARRASSING STORY?

When I was about nine I allowed some girls we'd been playing with to make me over for fancy dress. The girls promised me that I looked like Adam Ant, but in actual fact I looked more like Toyah Wilcox. This was made worse by the fact that I then had to walk all the way home in full, New Romantic garb.

SOMETHING NOBODY KNOWS ABOUT YOU:

I got engaged on live TV.

Foreword

Marketing today is hard. That's an inescapable truth and one that many businesses are struggling to overcome.

We used to live in a world where display ads had a click through rate of 10%; those same ads are now lucky if they get a click through rate of 0.10%. Whether it's unsubscribing from email lists, installing ad blockers or simply not answering the phone, consumers today have many options for blocking out our marketing.

This shift in power is not a bad thing for marketers. In fact, it's empowering. We have an opportunity in front of us to rethink how we treat our prospective customers. No longer just a metric in our spreadsheets, now we can provide them with some real and tangible value.

And therein lies the problem – creating real value. Traditional marketing is centred on the goals of the marketer, not those of the customer. How can we create a marketing experience that is tailored to the needs of our customers when we've never really considered who they are?

Hundreds of brands are vying for these customers' attention online. With a limited amount of attention to distribute among them, many brands are going to lose out, buried in the noise. How are you going to ensure your value is heard? Today your marketing needs to turn heads. It needs to provoke questions, stimulate conversations and generate a base of loyal followers. It's hard right? Marketing today is no cakewalk. Luckily, in *Getting Goosebumps* Bryan and Dave provide us with a blueprint that answers these questions, and it starts with 'Goosebumps'.

'Goosebumps' is what happens when you truly understand your audience and deliver real value to them. Goosebumps are the reason a new person will sign up to your email list, follow you on Twitter or Facebook and comment on your latest blog post.

What Bryan and Dave describe as 'goosebumps' should be one of the key metrics in your marketing today. It may not be easily summarised in a monthly report, but it will help you create an army of loyal followers for your products and services, one that doesn't simply disappear when you stop paying for advertisements. Marketing can seem complex at times, but it can also be extremely simple.

The brand with the most loyal followers will usually beat their competitors into submission. As a marketer you will never be asked to stop generating more traffic and leads. You will always be asked for more. It's what makes the great marketers, well, great. But should we always want 'more'? And are we making the best use of this 'more'? Well not without context.

Context is what helps us show the right content to the right audience at the precise moment it really matters to them. It's this context that will help you create a marketing funnel that is truly relevant to the individuals who are moving through it. Remember, these are people, not metrics in a spreadsheet. You want to create an experience that matters to them. Bryan and Dave describe how you can do this by creating a 'See Think, Do, Delight' funnel for your business.

Oh, this all sounds pretty simple right? But you're thinking, my audience isn't even seeing the content I'm creating for them. Yes, content marketing has literally exploded over the past three years. The competition for eyeballs is fierce. That's why the distribution of that content is so important. In chapter 7 we get an incredible list of tactics that will help us leverage social channels to help our content rise above the noise. In the following pages you will not only be introduced to an array of clever marketing concepts and tactics, but more importantly you will have some 'aha!' moments. Do you know the Hollywood formula that will help you create amazingly successful content? Have you considered why your marketing needs to appeal to both the 'human' and 'chimp' side of your customer's brain? Or why Red Bull's phenomenal marketing should have really been done by an insurance company, if insurance marketers had any balls!

But forget all that, here is the best thing about the book. It has been baked to perfection by the experience of two renowned marketers who have been there and done that. Bryan and Dave know what they're talking about. They aren't simply regurgitating some bland marketing theory that just sounds good. Instead, what they describe in the book actually works because they have implemented these strategies to help real companies build marketing and sales funnels that have helped to propel their business ahead of the competition. Simply put, these guys have walked the walk.

I hope you enjoy reading *Getting Goosebumps* as much as I did. I am confident that by implementing Bryan and Dave's concepts you are likely to redefine how you do marketing. Expect better results, more closed leads, delighted customers… as well as a lot of fun along the way.

Kieran Flanagan – Marketing Director, HubSpot
Follow Kieran on Twitter **@SearchBrat**

"Business is finally realising that these days, the talent holds the cards. The talent community is asking for more and different engagement from employers so that they can make better career choices. A strong employer brand brings that engagement."

"If you want your business to be competitive you need the best people to join you. You need to engage the talent market as you would engage with your customers. Employer brand is a shift in behaviour but businesses need to embrace it, empower their teams at every level and tell stories about their business and culture that cut through the noise."

"In working with Bryan and the team at Ph.Creative we enjoyed a lot of exponential learning. Marketing and recruitment came together to create focused personas for the talent we wanted to attract. Together we created an employer brand that successfully engaged with the talent we need to work towards solving some of the biggest problems society is facing."

Jon Stanners, is Head of Global Talent Engagement and Employer Brand at Alpha, a stealth moonshot facility based in Barcelona. It is funded by Telefonica to explore long-term innovation with exponential technologies, to solve some of the world's biggest social problems.
www.alpha.company

What is inbound marketing?

Inbound marketing is widely acclaimed as the most effective approach to digital marketing in the modern age. But we think it's much more than that.

Inbound marketing is a philosophy: a mindset that puts your audience first. For the first time in business history, it's the customer that is in control – not brands or businesses.

Inbound marketing is the smart, authentic approach to modern day brand and business building. Turning the traditional sales process on its head, inbound marketing focuses on pulling your customers in, rather than pushing your sales message out. It's an approach that compels you to dovetail your marketing planning with your business' aims and objectives, creating a seamless, consistent voice.

After all, it's much easier to grow a business if your prospects call up and buy from you, instead of you calling your prospects and trying to sell to them. Building a reputation and online following lets you begin to generate traffic, leads and new business. It's the approach which can help you side-step, reduce or eradicate costly digital display advertising entirely.

This book does not promise overnight success; inbound marketing takes effort, time and commitment. If you buy into the philosophy, this book will provide the insight, tools and resources to grow your business in a way that your audience not only appreciates, but is increasingly demanding.

What is talent attraction?

Talent attraction is essentially just marketing. However, instead of finding new customers, the messages, stories and budget are all focused towards finding new potential employees. Just like regular marketing, this practice is also made up of multiple strategies and tactics designed to draw talent toward an organisation for both immediate needs and prospecting for the future.

Since the early 2000s, the world of recruitment has slowly shifted away from a traditional, transactional approach for two main reasons – cost and, more importantly, to improve the brand experience for the candidate. The key shift is the realisation that candidates no long 'apply' for jobs, as much as 'shop' for jobs - they have more control than before, especially in industries or economic climates where they are in high demand.

Just like regular marketing before it, talent attraction has become – and continues to become – more and more sophisticated, as the marketplace becomes more competitive. As brands start to realise that finding the right talent is key to their growth – or even just their survival – the level of planning and detail has evolved significantly. Now, more than ever, developing a strong employer brand and translating that into an effective employee value proposition is essential – just like understanding the features of benefits of products and services in the marketing department.

Why this book will
help your business

You live in an online world. You wouldn't have got this far in Getting Goosebumps, otherwise. We know that this book will help 99.9% of people who sell products, services or their brand online - or anyone who wants to work in an organisation that does.

So, if you want to start, improve, or update your techniques for creating a compelling story to give your business a boost online, then read on... Here's how we'll help:

CEOs and business leaders
Looking to get a grip of how to direct digital communications with confidence and authority? This book will quickly empower you in how to command a disruptive and contagious future. This will strike a chord and sit by the bedside for weeks and weeks.

Senior marketing management
Looking to stretch a budget, find new ways to win and accelerate toward promotion? Following the principles in this book will help you stand out as an expert team leader, capable of challenging convention and inspiring a team towards award-winning work.

Marketing executives
Looking to stand out in a competitive team? Getting Goosebumps will keep you on the straight and narrow. It's a compass that's always pointed towards doing a good job properly first time – even under the pressures of a fast-paced agency.

SME business owners
Looking to punch above your weight, outsource to an agency with confidence and clarity and generate a significant ROI? This book gives you a solid grounding in the fundamentals of inbound marketing, so you can ask for what you want, and know exactly what you're getting.

Budding digital execs and trainees
Looking to impress a new team or climb the ranks quickly? Getting Goosebumps shows you how to approach a challenge from a different angle and come up with something that might just be truly remarkable.

Traditional marketers

Worried you've been left behind and looking for a guiding hand? This book will deliver the instant reassurance that your existing skills are very much in play, but will provide you with the additional principles to become contagious and magnetic in the dawning digital age.

The bedroom marketer

Looking for a way to cut through the noise and make sure you put your best foot forward? This book discusses the latest techniques and agency tips to make sure you're up-to-date and ready to tackle any challenge.

Head of talent attraction

Looking for a robust means of finding and attracting the best talent to your business? Want to reduce your cost and time to hire, as well as increasing the calibre and culture fit of those you attract? What about getting to know your audience so well, you can reduce the number of mis-matched applicants, because you actually start to repel those people that wouldn't thrive in your company?

This book will provide you with all of that and more.

How to read this book

We've included detailed download plans, so you can plot your step-by-step strategy in a detailed, measurable way. If you're following the Goosebumps strategy, we'd suggest reading the book through before you download the extras, so you know what you've got to do and when. If, of course, you're just looking for a little inbound inspiration, then don't feel you have to follow everything we say to the letter - just reading through some of the ideas and examples will help you clarify your planning.

Introduction

Imagine a simple and effective approach to marketing that delights your audience, and is driven directly by your business objectives.

By sharing our marketing philosophy with you, we aim to provide you with a means to simplify marketing again, putting the emphasis back on the customer and their experience, whilst driving action from the top line objectives of your business.

In order to achieve this we need to forget about technology for a second and think about human engagement – it's time to measure marketing using goosebumps.

We will inspire you to listen to and love your audience, that's the only way you'll truly out-think your competition. We want to empower you to create compelling marketing material that helps you build contagious messages and create a magnetic brand.

Every decision to buy is based on emotional triggers, so the best possible response to marketing material that you can ever hope for (right before your audience decides what action to take) is to get goosebumps.

Goosebumps: The physical, involuntary, telltale sign that an emotional connection has been made.

Getting goosebumps is the telltale sign that you are achieving a positive response from your audience. Without a great story to tell or a powerful message that lands with impact, all the tools and technology are irrelevant.

A passionate message delivered with impact will allow your audience to connect with your core vision and become an advocate for your business. That's what you should be aiming for, every time.

So let's start at the end. The foldout on the following pages is what your online marketing plan for 2018 could look like.

Most online marketing plans go wrong when they lack strategy and rely on general content and activity. Potential customers are quickly lost when brands create a set of rigid messages that only speak to one specific group, at a particular point in their buying cycle.

 Keep going

STRATEGIC GOALS FOR THIRD QUARTER
1. Release a new service
2. Sign up 100 additional brokers

STRATEGIC GOALS FOR FOURTH QUARTER
1. Investigate new verticals/opportunities
2. Increase renewals by 20%

Winning Themes

Winning Themes

ew service promotion	Benefits for brokers	Social promotion	Thought leadership style content	Email marketing	Big data
July	August	Septemeber	October	November	December

Twitter Deal/offer

Email Welcome email

her offer

Email Referral incentive

	July		August		Septemeber		October		November		December
followers	7000	Twitter followers	8000	Twitter followers	9000	Twitter followers	11k	Twitter followers	12k	Twitter followers	13k
e Views	4000	Youtube Views	4500	Youtube Views	5000	Youtube Views	6000	Youtube Views	6500	Youtube Views	7000
e traffic	90k	Website traffic	105k	Website traffic	110k	Website traffic	140k	Website traffic	160k	Website traffic	180k
r of leads	800	Number of leads	1200	Number of leads	1400	Number of leads	1800	Number of leads	2000	Number of leads	2500
er of sales	210	Number of sales	240	Number of sales	300	Number of sales	450	Number of sales	500	Number of sales	600
f sales	£52k	Value of salesv	£60k	Value of sales	£75k	Value of sales	£112	Value of sales	£125k	Value of sales	£150k

STRATEGIC GOALS FOR FIRST QUARTER	STRATEGIC GOALS FOR SECOND QUARTER
1. Increase leads by 20%	1. Increase referral acquisitions by 20%
2. Increase social engagement by 30%	2. Increase search engine rank

Winning Themes **Winning Themes**

Home improvements	Tips/advice month	Interactive content	Incentives	Service specific content	User generated content
January	February	March	April	May	June

Snapchat video

Youtube video

Youtube video

Website Blog post

See

Think

Do

Delight

Twitter Infographic

LinkedIn Blog post

Twitter Vou

	January		February		March		April		May		June	
Twitter followers	500	Twitter followers	1500	Twitter followers	3000	Twitter followers	5500	Twitter followers	6000	Twitter followers	7000	Twitter
Youtube Views	500	Youtube Views	1000	Youtube Views	1500	Youtube Views	2000	Youtube Views	2500	Youtube Views	4000	Youtub
Website Traffic	25k	Website traffic	30k	Website traffic	35K	Website traffic	40k	Website traffic	50k	Website traffic	90k	Websit
Number of leads	200	Number of leads	300	Number of leads	500	Number of leads	530	Number of leads	550	Number of leads	700	Numb
Number of sales	40	Number of sales	70	Number of sales	100	Number of sales	120	Number of sales	130	Number of sales	200	Numb
Value of sales	£10k	Value of sales	£17k	Value of sales	£25k	Value of sales	£30k	Value of sales	£32k	Value of sales	£50k	Value

⬅ Open

Persona 2:
Steven Wakefield

Steven is a 37 year old who has a top flight job working as Head of Corporate Affairs for a multi-national based in Central London. He is married with 2 children, owns his own home in London and likes to play gold. He spends a little time on Twitter and LinkedIn and browses YouTube at the weekends.

Steven's primary goals:
Steven's primary goal is to provide a high standard of living for his family. A long-term secondary goal is to save towards buying a holiday home abroad.

Steven's pain points:
Steven is time poor and very busy and finds complicated or convoluted processes annoying. If he has to re-read something to understand it he feels his time is being wasted. His main worry when purchasing a home insurance policy is getting stuck mid-way through an application with no one to help him. He wants to find a reputable insurer that can provide a tailored service to his specific needs, based on the sheer value of the goods he is insuring.

Keywords sets

See:
- Home insurance
- Home insurance quotes

Think:
- Home and contents insurance
- High value contents insurance

Do:
- Compare home insurance
- Comprehensive home insurance

Delight:
- Home insurance quotes
- Cheap house insurance

Persona empathy

See:
- Efficient
- Quick

*Inspire

Think:
- Valuables
- High-value

*Educate

Do:
- Compare
- Comprehensive

*Convince

Delight:
- Reviews
- Offers

*Inspire & convince

This old-school approach to digital marketing is dead. In order to succeed online, your digital strategy cannot be one size fits all. Your audience is made up of groups of individuals with distinct needs and expectations of your business. You must talk to them as if it's a one-on-one conversation wherever possible.

Remarkable online marketing today is fluid, yet targeted. It aligns with your business objectives and talks to your audience in a tailored way so as to maximise their experience with your brand. At every stage of your audience's buying cycle their needs, wants and desires change and you have to react accordingly. This might sound tough, but it's certainly not mission impossible and this book will prove it to you.

Untangling the elements of creating a robust, flexible and effective digital marketing strategy, this book will introduce eight fundamental principles that will ensure your business is always one step ahead online.

Behind each step in Getting Goosebumps you'll discover the latest agency secrets; mapping out exactly how to deliver creativity under pressure, without the worry that it's not contributing to the overall business numbers that matter.

See, think, do, delight

Persona 1
Paul Gerrard

Paul is 19 and is currently in his first year of university, studying law. He loves fashion, football and his friends and most of his buying decisions are motivated by convenience and price. He uses Snapchat and Twitter every day and watches YouTube and Netflix religiously.

Paul's primary goals:
Paul's primary goal is to retain as much of his money as possible for socialising. He is motivated by referral deals and incentives for signing up with a particular insurer.

Paul's pain points:
Paul doesn't own anything of significant value, so home insurance seems unnecessary to him; he views it as an expense he could do without. However, Paul listens to his parents when it comes to making new life decisions and he promised them that he would get contents insurance at a good price now that he has moved to university. The idea of filling out lengthy and complicated insurance forms is a real turn off for Paul.

Keywords sets

See:
- Cheap contents insurance
- Basic student insurance

Think:
- Cheap contents insurance
- Cheap insurance with cash back

Do:
- Compare cheap insurance
- Compare student insurance

Delight:
- Student content insurance
- Cheap contents insurance quote

Persona empathy

See:
- Cheap
- Basic

*Attract & Inspire

Think:
- Price
- Deals

*Educate

Do:
- Compare
- Cheapest

*Convince

Delight:
- Discounts
- Offers

*Reward & Inspire

"It is widely understood th
are emotional decisions. H
important to recognise the
and logical information to
decisions."

t all marketing decisions
owever, it is also
need for rational thinking
eaffirm those emotional

GETTING YOUR STORY STRAIGHT

Why it's important to you and your customers and how to ensure you're being authentic.

"A brand for a company is like a reputation for a person. You earn reputation by trying to do hard things well."
Jeff Bezos

"Great companies that build an enduring brand have an emotional relationship with customers that have no barrier. And that emotional relationship is based on the most important characteristic."
Howard Schultz

"Those are my principles, and if you don't like them... well, I have others."
Groucho Marx

Our philosophy is built around the belief that you need to weave interesting stories around your brand to emotionally connect with your intended audience. The world of marketing is changing and people are willing to be riveted, engaged with and moved by a story before they even consider engaging in business with your brand.

Your goal is to have them fall in love with you... Or at least create a brand-crush with lasting sentiment. One such example springs to mind; picture the scene.

Muharrem is deaf and communicates solely through sign language. Every day is spent trying to overcome barriers to communication and make meaningful sense of the everyday world. When we meet him, Muharrem is setting out one morning, accompanied by his sister Ozlem for a stroll through the quiet Istanbul suburb they both live in. When Muharrem bumps in to a stranger on the street, he discovers the first clue that today is no ordinary day. Muharrem is pleasantly surprised when that stranger signs 'good morning' to him.

Brushing the unlikely event off as a happy coincidence, Muharrem and Ozlem carry on through the streets, signing idle chat while heading towards a local food store. When the shopkeeper offers him hot bagels in sign language, and a customer who drops a bag of fruit on the floor apologies in the same way, the look of bemusement that washes over Muharrem's face reveals his racing mind and state of confusion.

"Do you know him? Is he hearing impaired?" he asks his sister.

"I don't know!"

Trying to adjust to the unfamiliar world in which he has suddenly found himself, Muharrem and Ozlem hail a cab. Of course, not everything is as it seems and the shock now fully floods Muharrem's face when the taxi driver cheerfully welcomes him and asks his destination in full, fluent sign language. All the barriers that Muharrem is used to navigating, every day of his life, are slowly melting away. Stepping out of the cab onto the local square Ozlem notices something from the corner of her eye.

"Look there! Look there!"

In the centre of the square was an electronic billboard, featuring an advert; pretty standard stuff for a bustling neighbourhood centre in a capital city. Except this billboard was using sign language. And it was signing directly to Muharrem.

"Hi Muharrem. Samsung wanted to prepare a little surprise for you because a world without barriers is our dream as well."

The day, of course, was not exactly as it seemed. Cameras swoop in on Muharrem as his sister, friends and bystanders embrace him. Muharrem had the chance to live for a day in a world without barriers thanks to a very special stunt from a brand that truly had its cause at the very heart of their marketing. Samsung Turkey took the residents from Muharrem's suburb of Istanbul (including his sister, who was in on it all along) and, in a single month, taught them all sign language. The tightly scripted and choreographed journey that Muharrem took was filmed by dozens of carefully concealed cameras as each participant joined in with the effort to help Muharrem spend a day in world where he could communicate with satisfaction and ease.

What for, you ask? Well, ultimately the stunt was aimed at advertising Samsung Turkey's new video-conferencing call centre for the hearing impaired. It's not a topic we can all relate to, but Samsung did something brilliant. They made a new call centre all about a human story. They found what they were all about, communication without barriers, and they engaged their audience in a story that perfectly reflected that value. Needless to say the corresponding video went viral, generating over 3 million views on YouTube (and counting) and became one of those clips that you just had to watch.

Regardless of how you feel about Samsung's new call centre, it's a day that you or Muharrem will not forget about any time soon and Samsung are that little bit more memorable for it too... You might have even developed a little soft spot in your heart for Samsung by the end of watching that video, or just like one of our team in Ph.Creative, you may find yourself in floods of tears (right Kathryn?).

Check it out by visiting the link below - we're sure it'll give you goosebumps.
ph-creative.com/Chapter1Resources

If you don't establish who you are and the reason you exist as a business, it's very difficult to convince any audience to trust you, buy from you or attach any loyalty toward your brand. On the other hand, if your purpose and your vision are clear, online communication can be an extremely powerful means of inspiring incredible storytelling and delivering a message that resonates with your audience.

The power of
getting it right

In December 2013 the eighth largest airline in America, WestJet Airlines, created a Christmas marketing campaign which not only generated a tonne of engagement, but it also demonstrated a brand that remains true to its values and vision.

WestJet Airlines has a vision: to become one of the biggest airlines in America by providing guests with a friendly, caring experience that redefines air travel. Their values include being honest, caring, positive and passionate in everything they do and keeping the commitments they make.

WestJet Airlines' Christmas Miracle campaign demonstrates a brand that cares about its customers. WestJet asked passengers what they wanted for Christmas before they boarded a flight, using an interactive Santa Claus TV screen. As each passenger scanned their boarding pass, Santa spoke to them personally to ask what they wanted for Christmas. It was a lovely touch of personal Christmas joy.

But that wasn't the end of the story. In the time it took the flight to take to the air from Toronto and reach its destination of Hamilton, WestJet had each and every customer's Christmas wish bought, gift wrapped and waiting for them at the other end on the luggage belt. Complete with a personal appearance from Santa.

WestJet has a reputation for looking after their employees and in return, they look after the details that delight their customers. So this stunt rings true with their brand story. It's heartwarming, personal, endearing and generous. It was documented and videoed, and its 36 million views on YouTube prove how successful it truly was.

This is an excellent example of strategic marketing that's in tune with the company's vision. Marketing magic can happen if your communications and marketing activities are all pulling in the same direction as your brand values, your vision and your purpose.

Plain old magic can happen every day too, but where WestJet Airlines succeeded is in maximising the potential of their campaign with clever marketing. They leveraged every bit of digital goodwill that was to be had from that particular marketing activity. There's nothing wrong with orchestrating this at all; it's not phoney, it's authentic.

WestJet Airlines live and breathe the sentiment behind the gesture which is why 36 million people have bought into the magic of the experience they created. They leveraged their purpose and their brand vision into an emotionally compelling stunt, and managed to execute it extremely well. See for yourself, it's marketing genius.

To access this video and all of your resources for chapter 1, visit the link below.
ph-creative.com /Chapter1Resources

What did you think? It's pretty compelling stuff. Now, we're aware that WestJet's campaign represents a big marketing campaign with an even bigger gesture. And of course, big gestures are often accompanied by big budgets. We understand that this kind of

marketing stunt may appear to be out of reach for many smaller businesses, but the key take away from the WestJet example is the concept and the intention.

Talking to your customers and listening to what they want will get you further than any mammoth marketing budget. You might not be able to give them flat screen TVs for Christmas, but you can give them a brilliant experience at every stage of the buying cycle. That gift is worth its weight in gold in the world of business.

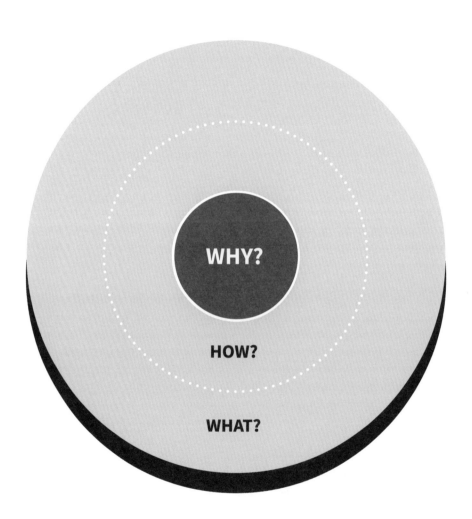

The science behind the approach

Are there certain brands that you just can't help but be enamoured with? Have you ever been won over by clever advertising or packaging? Have you ever listened to a keynote speech by a CEO or business owner and been inspired? Let's be honest – we all have.

Simon Sinek, author of Start with Why sums up why some brands make a connection and others miss the mark by introducing the idea of 'The Golden Circle'. Three concentric circles, decreasing in size represent three questions; what, how and why?

What?

The 'what' represents the services and products you sell.

How?

The 'how' represents the way you make your products/services.

Why?

The 'why' is the rationale behind everything you do as a business.

It's the 'why' stage that is so often glossed over when planning brand communications and online activities – the stumbling block for many businesses.

The success of global brands such as Innocent, Starbucks and Apple is that they always start with 'why' and then take you on the emotional journey of what their products stand for.

We understand the purpose and beliefs of these brands and we're instantly provided with a means of emotionally investing in them. So, what's your purpose? Why should your audience emotionally invest in your brand? How can you use your higher purpose to inspire, entertain, educate and convince them to stay loyal?

The consequences of getting it wrong

Not all brands are quite as savvy as WestJet, Starbucks or Apple. Even global powerhouses can fall when they fail to understand both what they say they stand for and what their target audience actually believe they represent.

Take investment bank J.P. Morgan. On its website it lists the following as one of its core values:

"We do our best to manage and operate our company with a consistent set of business principles. We believe that shareholders will benefit as we do the right thing for our clients and the communities we serve."

So what happened in 2013, when the bank invited Twitter followers to ask Vice Chairman Jimmy Lee anything, in an enlightening Q&A session, using the hashtag #AskJPM?

Six hours of carnage is the answer. Twitter users questioned and condemned everything from the bank's role in the financial crisis and why no-one has been held accountable, to their involvement in the Bernie Madoff investment scandal.

Ultimately and unsurprisingly the Twitter Q&A was cancelled. This PR disaster could have been avoided if their online communication was rooted in a robust strategy, informing them of what their brand actually represents to the masses on the internet.

By failing to understand their online brand perception, and for jumping into an online activity without prior research, they jeopardised their brand even further.

J.P. Morgan could have avoided this if they had incorporated a blended approach to their PR and social media; by tuning in to the conversations their audience were having and responding to their concerns, rather than jumping on a trend in a bid to appear relevant.

The moral of the story? Live and breathe your brand values online, or you'll get caught out. Ensure your mission statement, vision and core values inform your online marketing strategy.

Opposite is a diagram for you to fill in, so you can note the 'what', 'how' and 'why' that make up your business. Start with why, then work your way through the sections. In the centre of the diagram, you should be able to form a set of tangible brand values that define your business based on the three principles.

You can download your own printable version of this worksheet at:
ph-creative.com/Chapter1Resources

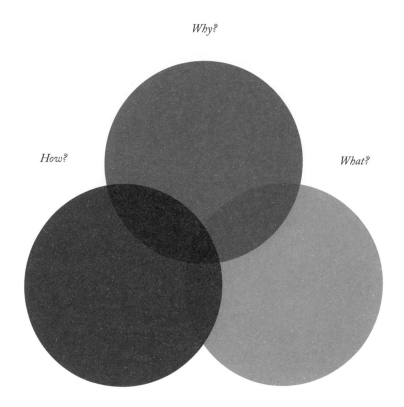

Why?

How?

What?

List your brand values

IF YOU REMEMBER
ONE LAST THING

**If your marketing team doesn't ensure your strategy aligns
with your brand's values and business objectives, how can
you be sure what you're doing online is authentic?**

And more importantly, how can you convince your customers
of this? To get goosebumps your audience must feel the
authenticity and believe your message to be true.

Recommended reading & resources

BOOKS

Fish!
Stephen Lundin
This management parable, set in the fishmongers at Seattle's Pike Place Market, sees protagonist Mary Jane Ramirez tasked with turning around her company's failing operations department. This book is designed to help find a way to create a fun, happy work place, where employees live and breathe the company's vision and values.

Creativity Inc.
Ed Cartmull
As much a history of Pixar as management book, this is a definitive guide to building a creative business. Cartmull's storytelling takes us through his journey to connect the many specific tasks his employees perform with Pixar's wider business objectives, driving his team to create such animated classics as Toy Story and Finding Nemo.

Start with Why: How Great Leaders Inspire Everyone to Take Action
Simon Sinek
This book outlines the 'Golden Circle' – the 'how?', 'what?' and 'why?' It advocates starting every business, project or campaign by asking 'why?' first. That way, you establish the reason for asking your audience for their loyalty.

ONLINE TOOLS

TinyPulse
This online system collects anonymous feedback from employees, creating a barometer of happiness in your organisation. You can choose pre-written questions or create your own, so you can delve into how much your team understands your vision and values.
tinypulse.com

The Feedback Matrix
The real impact of feedback, positive or negative, comes in the manner you respond to it – or indeed if you choose to respond at all. First ask yourself 'what can I do with this criticism/compliment?' Create and plot feedback on a matrix divided into four sections: advice, compliments, criticism and suggestions, then decide what advice to follow, what to ignore and what should drive you to take action.

Brand values guidelines download

Download our brand values guidelines template by visiting the link below to start effectively building the framework for your business and planning your goals accordingly.

ph-creative.com/Chapter1Resources

Takeaways for chapter 1

Now that we've explored the importance of understanding how your brand values affect the way your audience perceives you, check off each of the stages below as you complete them.

☐ Establish what you stand for

☐ Decide how you want your audience to view you

☐ Set a clear message

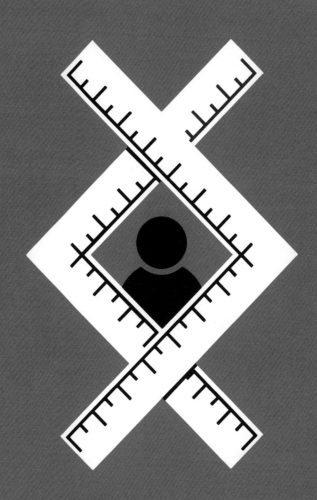

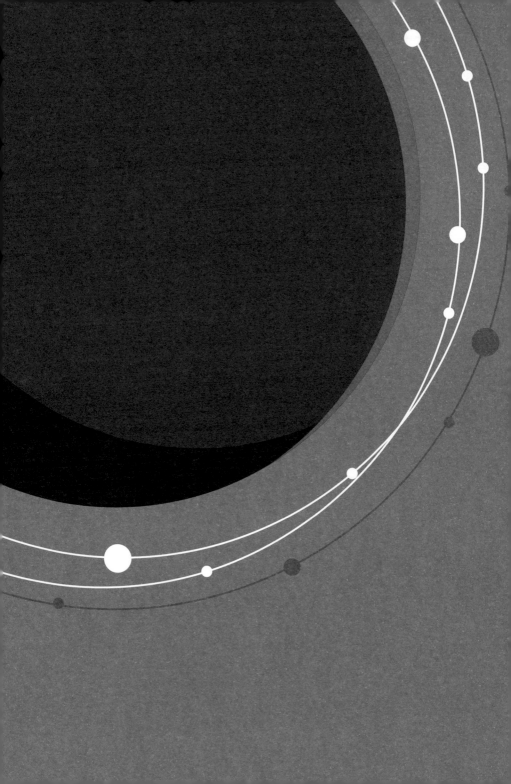

THE RIGHT DIRECTION

How to align your business objectives with your marketing goals to ensure everyone in the business is on the same page.

"Strategy is buying a bottle of fine wine when you take a lady out for dinner. Tactics is getting her to drink it."
Frank Muir

"Victorious warriors win first and then go to war, while defeated warriors go to war first and then seek to win."
Sun Tzu, The Art of War

"A satisfied customer is the best business strategy of all."
Michael LeBoeuf

All too often, there are three scenarios that play out when businesses plan their online activities.

The first scenario occurs when there is no strategy whatsoever. Instead, a handful of well-meaning tactics and activities are routinely or sporadically executed in the hope that online magic will happen, more leads will find their way to the business, and sales will drop through the till each month.

The second scenario is sometimes more dangerous than the first. There is a digital strategy in place yet it doesn't integrate with the overarching goals of the business. Instead, it resembles a collection of generic tactics and social media measurables, and as a result fails to add any value to the current business objectives.

The third scenario occurs when a digital strategy has been designed with the business objectives in mind, however on review, it's now either drifted into a more diluted version of the original vision or it's stuck too rigidly to the original plan – even though the business has now moved in a new direction.

All of these scenarios are symptoms of the same root cause. A digital strategy, plan or routine of activity is sometimes the afterthought of a business strategy that sees digital as merely a tactic or an amplification technique for existing activities.

Digital can certainly extend reach, stretch conversion rates and help to increase audience engagement, however digital should be used strategically and not just tactically.

Writing your
digital strategy

If you don't know why you are doing something, how can you set real goals and measurable Key Performance Indicators (KPIs) to work towards? How can you identify if what you are doing is working?

Asking 'why' will help you to identify your business objectives, which in turn will form the foundation of your every activity online – helping you to build a clear strategic timeline or plan to follow.

Identify the 'why' and your strategic plan will follow. Plotting activities on a chart and then asking yourself – 'why are we doing this? Does this align with our overall business objectives?' – will ensure you generate real, tangible results.

The Ph.Creative methodology enables you to plan your communications and inbound marketing by starting with why.

It's this approach that means you're not flailing around in the tactics and activity of social media without adding value to your business goals. An effective strategic plan has to be:

S pecific

M easurable

A cheivable

R elevant

T imely

Setting 'SMART' objectives is a method as old as the hills, but 'SMART' objectives are still the best starting point when defining your business' goals.

- Write down your specific objective
- Outline how you will measure it
- Check it is attainable and relevant to your company's vision
- Set a deadline for when this should be achieved

Download our SMART objectives marketing goals template by visiting the link below to start planning your business goals with clarity. **ph-creative.com/Chapter2Resources**

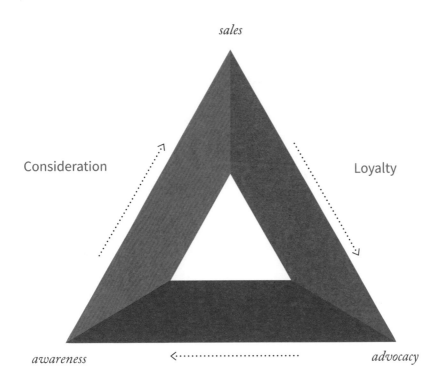

Sales – Advocacy – Awareness

These are three metrics that should always play a part in your business objectives. Use this model to ensure you focus on one primary objective, integrating the others throughout.

Examples of digital strategy at work

Once you've laid out your KPIs and ascertained why you're doing what you're doing, you can start putting a strategy together that is in-line with the primary objectives of your business.

Below are some good examples of a digital strategy at work:

- Growing a Facebook community of 100,000 engaged fans because you consistently convert an average of 13% of the community with every promotion.

- Driving revenue up by 5% by increasing the conversion rate of your website by 5% and the traffic by 25%.

- Using regular email marketing to nurture a list of prospects towards buying for the first time. Convert 90% of first time customers into repeat customers by refining a follow-up email campaign.

- Finding and targeting social 'influencers' to build reputation and credibility in a specialist field.

- Engaging a new persona of your audience worth an additional 10% of gross profit.

"Convert 90% of first time customers into repeat customers."

Considering your
digital tactics

So where does it usually go wrong? Among the success stories from brands and companies using social media are many more failures, often rooted in the fact that objectives for each channel were not planned out from the start. Here are four of the most common.

'Let's sell on Twitter'

Many businesses use channels like Twitter effectively to engage with customers. But when used without clear objectives in mind, it can be detrimental to your brand.

Today's consumers expect brands to work to win trust and provide value online, not just lead with a sales pitch.

Being overly pushy with your sales tactics on this platform can backfire, ultimately losing you followers (and potential customers). Similarly, posting content to Twitter without prior knowledge of your audience personas will also result in lower engagement and follower rate.

'The target audience online is the same as it is offline'

Targeting the same people online as offline is not always the best method to employ. When setting digital objectives you need a clear understanding of how your audience will interact with you online, so you can target them effectively.

Individuals often have different habits on and offline – a customer who may buy exclusively in store won't respond to a sales message asking them to purchase online and vice versa.

It's also important to think about how your target audience shops online – whether they need information first or are driven by sales or discounts.

'We'll just have an infographic'

Just throwing a piece of content out into the digital space and hoping someone will see it is useless. Content such as infographics and blogs need to be backed by a relevant strategy based on clearly defined objectives. One problem that occurs often is the promotion of content becoming an afterthought.

You may have the best infographic or blog article in the world, but if you're only sharing it with your 400 Facebook followers, your reach will be severely hindered.

'That campaign was great, thanks, bye'

Inbound marketing doesn't stop after one campaign or even at the checkout button. Setting an objective to continue building relationships will open doors for up-selling and retaining loyal customers.

If you continue to delight your customers after the initial sale, you'll create a community of active brand ambassadors and advocates who endorse, support and ultimately love your brand.

Defining your objectives

You and your team should be on the pulse of emerging media; new platforms, techniques and tools – but that doesn't mean you should cram them all into your marketing programme. Carefully select only the channels and metrics that will benefit your business.

Once you've outlined clear SMART goals and objectives and mapped out your personas, selecting the right channels should fall naturally into your tactics.

Ensure you consistently review these however, if your personas' interests and online habits change - don't get left behind.

Six metrics to consider when
defining tactics

Reputation

Create an enhanced experience, valuable content or great customer service and your reputation will build trust, encourage advocacy and generate customer referrals.

Engagement

Authentic, honest engagement with your customers will drive trust and advocacy. The more you engage, the more your customers will teach you about your brand, informing your objectives.

Awareness

Raising brand visibility in the digital space is not an easy task. With so many competitors vying for your audience's attention, being seen can prove difficult. Setting this as a key objective and pinpointing where your customers are and what they want to see will ensure you remain visible in the online space.

Sales

Encouraging your audience to give their details and permission to market to them allows you to remain in contact with them and personalise your approach.

Sentiment

Through enhanced navigation and customer service online, your brand can provide value and a great experience, improving sentiment and encouraging referrals and re-visits.

Visibility

Ranking for the right keywords is still relevant. Know what your audience is searching for and make sure you're in a high position when they make that search.

Examples of digital
tactics at work

The tactics you implement should have the primary focus of achieving your strategy and meeting the goals you originally laid out for your business.

Below are some good examples of digital tactics at work:

- Using Facebook to invite people to a seminar

- Using Google Adwords to find more customers searching for your products or services right now

- Emailing your database to market a 50% off January sale

- Tweeting every time there's news or a new blog released on the website

- Sending sales 'In-Mails' on LinkedIn to ideal prospects, city by city

Remember, your strategic list should focus on achieving your business goals, while your tactical list should be your to-do list for the month.

Before executing digital tactics, a clear strategy must be established that's in-line with the primary objectives of the business. The good news is that this doesn't have to be difficult at all.

**IF YOU REMEMBER
ONE LAST THING**

**Before you do anything, define effective, meaningful objectives that will make
an impact on your business and resonate with your customers.**

Use our strategy worksheet at the end of this chapter to help you define these.
Combine your tactics with your strategy and above all, remember to connect with
your customers on an emotional level.

If you can successfully communicate your 'cause' or your 'why' (what you stand for
over and above a financial gain) you provide something they can believe in and
champion with you.

If you achieve this, goosebumps aren't far away.

Recommended reading & resources

BOOKS

Breakthrough! How Great Companies Set Outrageous Objectives - And Achieve Them Bill Davidson
Although not strictly an inbound marketing text, this book looks at more than 70 breakthrough brands, including IBM, Dell and American Standard and shows how they adopted outrageous objectives and what happened when they achieved them.

Mastering the Rockefeller Habits Verne Harnish
This book champions prioritisation and will help you to identify what's critical for you to achieve in the next 90 days, helping you communicate it to your team, creating energy and focus.

ONLINE TOOLS

Google Analytics
Google Analytics is an essential tool in understanding your website traffic sources, ecommerce goals, search terms and audience demographics.
google.com/analytics

Dash This
Dash This makes your reporting tasks simple, and pulls information from a range of sources. Allowing you to create weekly, monthly, quarterly and annual reports and providing an instant snapshot of your performance, Dash This is a great tool to add to your armoury.
dashthis.com

Implementing your brand values download

Download our guide to implementing your brand values by visiting the link below to start effectively incorporating your values into your content strategy.

ph-creative.com/Chapter2Resources

Takeaways for chapter 2

Now you understand how to set achievable goals and the key differences between tactics and strategy, there are a few things you should do to ensure you maximise your success rate. Check them off below as you complete them.

☐ Cement your business objectives

☐ Link each tactic within your strategy to your business objectives

☐ Check your strategy against the SMART method

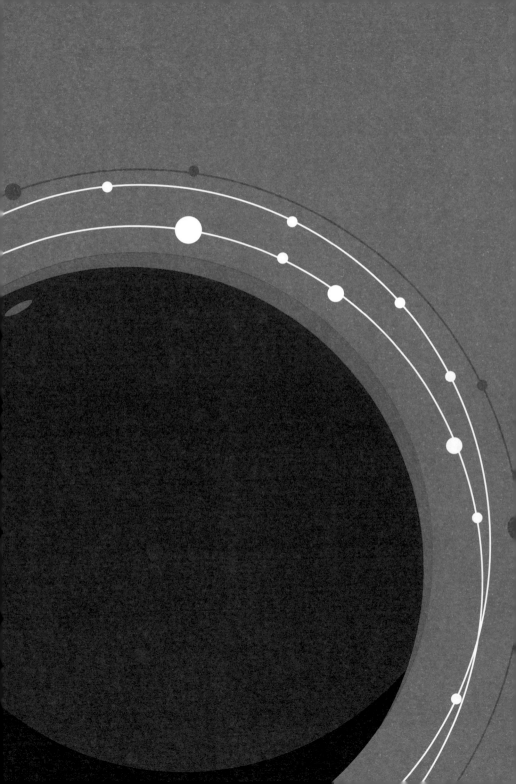

UNDERSTANDING YOUR AUDIENCE

How to listen to your audiences' wants, needs and desires in order to maximise your chances of engaging and selling to them.

"The aim of marketing is to know and understand the customer so well that the product or service fits him and sells itself."
Peter Drucker

"When you enchant people, your goal is not to make money from them or get them to do what you want but to fill them with great delight."
Guy Kawasaki

"The attention economy is not growing which means we have to grab the attention that someone else has today."
Brent Leary, CRM Essentials

So, the search for goosebumps continues. This chapter is make or break for our cause because it's here that you will decide on the answer to the following crucial question. How much do you really want to make that connection with your audience?

Have you ever heard the saying, 'people buy from people they like'? This is an old adage, which has been written about and quoted many times over the years – especially in books and white papers written about sales techniques and tactics. It stands to reason that in order to be effective with sales and marketing, you need to understand your audience, their motivations for buying and what's important to them – not so you can use creepy sales techniques, but so you can give them the value they're looking for and make their life easier.

By understanding the ways in which your products or services address a pain point or common problem for your audience, you're ensuring that your content is always relevant, valuable and isn't trying to force a sale.

The quickest and most effective way to achieve this is to fully understand your audience and, at the risk of sounding a little mushy, you've got to also love them enough to want to understand what matters to them most. You need to get a grip on what your audience really appreciate and act on this to build a meaningful relationship – one that's based on value and trust.

The world has changed and the power has most definitely shifted between consumer and business brand. It's no longer relevant or acceptable to use over-bearing persuasion techniques that border on manipulation to hammer home your sales messages. Instead, the consumer dictates that we lead with value and play by their rules on their terms.

Our professional duty is to live up to this expectation and optimise the user experience. Thus, maximising conversions, from passive engagement to a qualified lead or sale. It could be argued that consumer behaviour and power has shifted so much that the art of ethical persuasion has become re-aligned with its original definition.

To become more effective with all aspects of marketing, we've experimented, tested and consulted a vast array of sources and experts over the years.

One simple message that we continue to revisit has been the idea that during an experience with your brand, people don't necessarily remember what you said (or wrote); instead, they remember how you made them feel. So, we're back to our original premise of, can you provoke goosebumps?

Or do you leave your audience cold despite conveying all of the relevant information? The art of persuading your audience involves considering three basic appeals; pathos, ethos and logos, which were originally defined by Aristotle. Who knew? The greatest inbound marketer of all time is Aristotle. Pathos, ethos and logos divide the methods of persuasion into three categories: personal character, emotion and logic respectively.

Using a blend of these appeals will ensure that your marketing always resonates with your audience and you consistently drive your customers through the sales funnel. They could also be the secret ingredients to Getting Goosebumps.

Pathos

Pathos considers a direct appeal to the emotions of your audience. By understanding your audience and mapping your ideal personas (semi-fictional representations of your ideal customer), you can gauge which emotions get the best result. Through fully understanding the pain points and pleasure triggers of your audience, you can connect on an emotional level. This will give them not only a reason to share your content, but a reason to form a bond with your brand – making them more likely to become advocates.

Of all the three appeals, it is pathos that is considered the most important to master and lead with, where possible and appropriate, in your marketing. All buying decisions are emotional, regardless of what it is being bought and if you know your audience well enough to make a connection, you will reap the rewards from a business perspective.

Ethos

Ethos is the appeal of credibility and personal character. By crafting ethos into your messages you are building and defining credibility through establishing authority and respect. Your marketing should convey the idea that you are a trustworthy brand and build a strong case for your character.

Logos

Logos is a logical appeal, typically marked by facts, figures and data. This kind of appeal helps your audience rationalise their buying decisions through showing them clear, logical benefits. The psychology of the buying decision dictates that your customer feels they have made the right choice in their purchase. Appealing to your persona's logical side by providing facts, data and reviews about your products or services acts as a form of social proof for your customer, cementing and reinforcing their decision to buy.

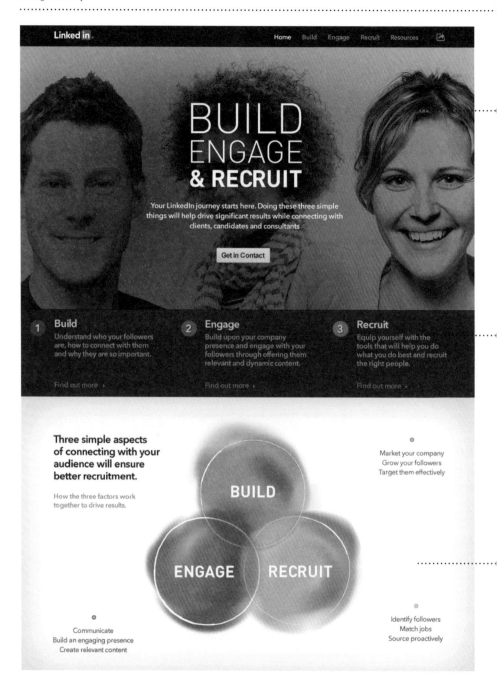

Pathos

Pathos is crafted into this webpage design through the introduction of relatable characters. This is achieved by the addition of photographs of the brand's key personas.

Ethos

Ethos is established within this webpage through the use of brand messaging. The benefits of LinkedIn are clearly spelled out for the user, which highlights the credibility of the brand.

Logos

Logos is achieved through presenting the key facts and figures and rational benefits of the service. The diagram, coupled with the accompanying copy helps the audience reinforce their decision to use the service.

Buyer personas

To make a true emotional connection with the members of our audience, we'd have to sit and meet each and every one of them. Whilst effective in the long term, it's not exactly scalable and possibly not the most sensible option for most businesses looking for goosebumps moments with their audience.

With this in mind, the practice of persona mapping can be extremely effective and a lot more practical!

Buyer personas identify common behavioural patterns, shared pain points, both professional and personal, as well as universal goals and the dreams of your customers. This provides a powerful bank of information which will enable you to deliver information, products and services that fit their needs.

HubSpot defines a buyer persona as the following:

'A buyer persona is a semi-fictional representation of your ideal customer based on market research and real data about your existing customers. When creating your buyer persona(s), consider including customer demographics, behaviour patterns, motivations, and goals. The more detailed you are, the better.'

Who should you ask about your buyer personas?

Don't just ask your sales team about your customers, this will give a one-dimensional result. Instead you should try to ask a range of people, including:

Your customers – through surveys, polls and focus groups

Potential customers who didn't buy (to find out why)

Senior team members – CEOs, Directors and Managers

Marketing executives

Sales team

This will give a broader, more balanced view of your personas.

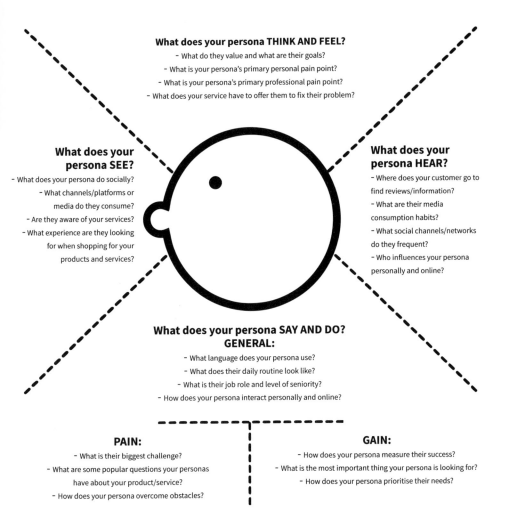

What does your persona THINK AND FEEL?
- What do they value and what are their goals?
- What is your persona's primary personal pain point?
- What is your persona's primary professional pain point?
- What does your service have to offer them to fix their problem?

What does your persona SEE?
- What does your persona do socially?
- What channels/platforms or media do they consume?
- Are they aware of your services?
- What experience are they looking for when shopping for your products and services?

What does your persona HEAR?
- Where does your customer go to find reviews/information?
- What are their media consumption habits?
- What social channels/networks do they frequent?
- Who influences your persona personally and online?

What does your persona SAY AND DO?
GENERAL:
- What language does your persona use?
- What does their daily routine look like?
- What is their job role and level of seniority?
- How does your persona interact personally and online?

PAIN:
- What is their biggest challenge?
- What are some popular questions your personas have about your product/service?
- How does your persona overcome obstacles?

GAIN:
- How does your persona measure their success?
- What is the most important thing your persona is looking for?
- How does your persona prioritise their needs?

Persona mapping

Once you've identified your buyer personas, there are eight actions that will help you to maximise this insight and generate real results for your business:

1. Reallocate your resources

Are most of your personas on Twitter? Take your executives off Facebook and move them onto Twitter. Is your online ad spend with LinkedIn, but your customers are on Facebook? Move your ad spend.

2. Use their language

Make sure your communication reflects their tone of voice. Use the buzzwords and slang they use and make sure you place yourself at the centre of their community.

3. Personalise communication

Segment contact lists by persona, so you can provide each with tailored content. That way, you won't alienate your customers with irrelevant news, information and offers.

4. Create content with your personas in mind

Whether it's a video, blog post or landing page, every piece of content you create should speak to one particular persona. Identify what engages, excites and entertains them and provide it!

5. Learn what your personas search for

Keywords still play a critical role in inbound marketing strategies. Identify the problems your personas want to solve and what they are searching for to help them find resolutions.

6. Audit your existing content

Look at your existing content and work out which persona it aligns with. If it doesn't speak to any of your buyer personas, rework it or – if it can't be updated – get rid of it.

7. Co-market with relevant brands

If you join forces with other brands that your personas admire, you'll double your power. Try a joint webinar with a media partner or invite an industry thought leader to guest blog for an instant boost.

8. Map your personas to the buying cycle

Pinpoint your customer's stage in the buying cycle (how close they are to purchase) so you can provide even more relevant and targeted content that will bring them closer to committing to buy.

Breaking down the customer journey

By identifying specific buyer personas within a business's audience, we can begin to explore the subtle (or sometimes not so subtle) differences in how we need to communicate a message, in order to get the desired response we're looking for.

To illustrate this point we've created an example company called Got It Covered Insurance (GICI). GICI sells home insurance to a variety of customers but has identified four different buyer personas that neatly categorise the majority of their audience and also represent who it feels they are most likely to sell to.

GICI's buyer personas are as follows:

1. Affluent home-owners in central London
2. Established landlords with a large portfolio
3. Housing associations
4. Students moving to university for the first time

Even at first glance, it is understandable that despite selling the exact same insurance product to each buyer persona, the message, tone of voice and the incentive or main calls to action will need to be different. By taking the time to understand each persona, we will soon see just how different those key messages need to be. The more information we can obtain for each persona, the better our results will be later down the line. Giving each persona a name, job, age and living scenario helps to fill in gaps that pay dividends when it comes to devising a content plan.

Mapping your personas based on their demographics and lifestyle is a good place to start, but doing something called empathy mapping your personas will help you dig deeper to uncover exactly what they think and feel. Empathy mapping is a technique that adds value and insight to the picture that you have already painted of your buyer personas. Your demographic research and impression of your target customer will tell you who they are. But empathy mapping tells you what they feel, how they think and in what ways they are most likely to act.

This is a tremendously useful process because it puts you in your potential buyers' shoes. It is this process that allows you to understand their pain points and what emotionally affects them and tailor your marketing messaging accordingly. Of course, this process needs validating with solid research, however most businesses are sat on this valuable information about their audience but they're just not putting it to good use. Take a look at the fictional personas on the next page. Do they seem reasonable to you? Given the information on hand, do the related strategic decisions that follow each one make sense? You be the judge.

Buyer persona one:

Affluent home-owners in central London

Demographics

Name: Steven Wakefield
Age: 37
Job title: Head of Corporate Affairs
Income: £75k (combined household income: £150k)
Home status: Home-owner, married, two small children
Education: Masters degree in Economics & History

Identifiers

- Methodical, diligent, thorough
- Appreciates quality and attention to detail
- Articulate, can be stubborn, likes to argue a point
- Is rarely impulsive but appreciates a good deal
- Likes golf and football
- Spends time during the week on Twitter, LinkedIn and occasionally browses YouTube at the weekends

Goals

- Primary goal is to provide a high standard of living for family
- Secondary goal is to save towards buying a holiday home abroad

How GICI helps

- Provides comprehensive, no nonsense cover that's competitively priced
- Makes it easy to add high value items to a premium without fuss and without huge increases in monthly payments
- Premium, fast-track claims membership makes it quick and simple to claim when necessary

What Steven appreciates most about GICI

- GICI offers a plain English, clear guide to what's covered and what's not
- It's easy to add items to the policy online without fuss
- GICI rewards Steven every year with a free case of wine for not making a claim and reminds him of the competitive rates he's paying compared to the general market place

Empathy map of Steven Wakefield

Steven considers his time to be valuable and has a high level of self-importance. He feels annoyed if instructions or explanations are not made simple because having to read over complicated information is a waste of time.

Steven appreciates a clear offer and upfront details of what the product includes and does not. He requires reassurance and confidence to submit a form online and will only do so if he's read and understood all of the information he's presented with.

He sees himself as a valuable customer to an insurance company because of the sheer value of the contents and goods he is insuring and he likes to feel appreciated and valued.

His main worry about approaching an insurance company online is getting mid-way through an application process and being stuck without anyone to help him. His main worry in general terms is making a claim and being turned down due to misinterpreting terms and conditions on application.

A further challenge for Steven is to find a reputable insurer that offers an efficient, tailored service based on his needs, that can provide the peace of mind of comprehensive contents cover which is inclusive of all of the valuable items in his home.

His desired outcome is to complete an efficient, yet thorough online process without the ambiguity or grey areas that plant seeds of doubt before processing the final application. Having a person on hand to answer any

questions, quickly and easily is a well-placed comfort blanket that motivates Steven to proceed from the start.

Ideal marketing messages / sign posts for Steven:

1. No hidden clauses: we insure all of your home contents for the price we agree. No fuss and no exceptions.

2. If you have any issues worries or doubts during your application process, an advisor is on hand to answer your questions and help you complete your application properly.

3. It takes six minutes from start to finish to fill in this simple application.

4. We provide a personal hotline to your dedicated relationship manager to deal with your every need without delay.

5. As a thank you, please enjoy a free case of wine of your choice now and every year you stay with us.

Buyer persona two:

Students moving to university for the first time

Demographics

Name: Paul Gerrard
Age: 19
Job Title: Student
Income: 12k
Home status: Renting, single, no dependents
Education: Pre-law

Identifiers

- Carefree, excitable, outgoing
- Loves fashion, football and friends
- Highly motivated by convenience
- Most buying decisions are made based on price
- Listens to his parents when it comes to new life decisions
- Uses Snapchat every day, watches YouTube and Netflix religiously and is just starting to watch and host Meerkat chats

Goals

- Primary goal: Retain as much disposable income for socialising a possible
- Secondary goal: See primary goal

How GICI Helps

- Takes care of everything quickly and easily
- Offers a one size fits all basic package
- Rewards Paul with a voucher for a supermarket

What Paul appreciates most about GICI

- The price is cheap
- He has a voucher to buy beer with immediately
- The promise to replace his phone or laptop within 24 hours of making a claim

Empathy map of Paul Gerrard

Paul doesn't own anything of significant value apart from a laptop, a smart phone and some household basics. Therefore, he sees home insurance as an expense he would rather do without. He is pretty carefree and can't imagine anything going wrong at home and so he would much rather spend his money on socialising and enjoying himself.

When he sees the voucher reward for signing up, Paul is drawn to the immediate gratification and could be persuaded to pass on the offer if there was a further reward for generating referrals amongst his friends.

He is fairly well educated, however he is laid back and likes to have a simple life. Complicated forms and lengthy paragraphs of text cause Paul to run for the hills and put off the job until tomorrow or never.

His top challenge is to please his parents by keeping the promise of getting home contents insurance whilst saving as much money as possible.

His desired outcome would be to complete a form in less than ten minutes and to have the entire process done, dusted and confirmed – including the voucher to claim £50 of goods at his local supermarket on the same day.

Ideal marketing messages / sign posts for Paul:
1. Sign up now for £120 and immediately receive a £50 voucher to spend in Tesco.
2. It takes less than ten minutes to complete the entire application process.

3. Refer a friend and receive a £20 voucher for every referral that signs up.
4. One price, no fuss.
5. Lose your phone and receive a replacement within 24hrs.

So, as you can see, the key messages are tailored to appeal to two different personas within the same audience, to provoke the best response. Although the product is the same, their needs are different and so should be the messaging.

I'm sure you'll agree, if those messages were diluted in order to speak to the audience as a whole, the chances of engagement would reduce dramatically. How can you expect to reach a 37 year old family man with the same marketing message used to reach an 19 year old student who has just moved away from home for the first time?

Given the insight into these two personas, let's quickly look at how that might influence our content plan, to reach each of them at each stage of the marketing funnel.

We'll cover how to design an efficient marketing funnel a little later on, however it's important you grasp the power of persona and empathy mapping and the power it gives you for getting goosebumps from your audience. Here's what a potential content journey might be to engage with Steven.

STEP ONE
Right at the top of the funnel. To get Steven to SEE the GICI brand and register their existence.

Channel: YouTube
Content type: Video
Intention: Inspire
Message: Our premium members enjoy luxury benefits including golf, spa, football and weekend breaks.

STEP TWO
Middle of the funnel. To get Steven to THINK about GICI as a possible solution to a specific need he has for insurance. Also create awareness of the GICI website.

Channel: Twitter
Content type: Infographic
Intention: Educate

Message: Compare detail, costs and benefits of the top 5 premium home insurance products on the market.

Channel: LinkedIn
Content type: Blog post(Pulse article)
Intention: Educate
Message: The networking and socialising benefits of joining exclusive B2B memberships and clubs.

STEP THREE
Near the bottom of the funnel. To entice Steven to DO something with GICI to either buy immediately or at least engage with the brand and input contact details.

Channel: Twitter
Content type: Deal/offer
Intention: Convince
Message: Register your interest in our home insurance premium this month for free exclusive membership to our club.

STEP FOUR
Right at the bottom the funnel. To DELIGHT Steven with an exceptional customer experience that he values enough to become a brand ambassador.

Channel: Email
Content type: Welcome email
Intention: Inspire and convince
Message: We're so pleased you've decided to join our club, we'd like to send you a bottle of wine to celebrate and invite you to join our private LinkedIn group where we share even more membership value.

In reality, Steven will bounce all over the internet and social channels, searching before he settles on GICI. He may even ask friends and find insight and be influenced by many other brands. However, with this approach, we're strategically putting content in the places he is most likely to see it and stacking the odds in our favour when it comes to reaching our target persona.

What's more, because we understand what Steven appreciates and responds to, we can tailor the style, tone and personality of the content to best match his wants, needs and desires.

We're also considering his frame of mind and where he might be in a buying/decision making cycle at that point in time. Content at the start of his journey is produced simply to entertain or inspire. Whereas later in his buying journey, content that is specifically designed to educate and convince is more useful and much more likely to have the desired effect.

If you're still not convinced, go back over Paul's persona details and then follow the same four steps we've outlined for Steven but replace the channel, content type, intention and the message to be more appropriate for Paul.

We guarantee that you will design a completely different path for Paul, and so you should.

By concentrating on getting the right content in the right places at the right time, you are creating a content infrastructure that will lead your audience down a well-designed marketing funnel that leads to more leads and sales. Imagine having a tailored audience journey for each of your personas and imagine what a difference it will make to your results when you do.

Persona mapping validation

Once you have taken a step towards getting to know your audience by mapping the specific needs, wants and desires of your various personas, you have automatically shot to the top of your class in our book and more than likely taken a giant step towards crushing your competition too.

However, without validating your research, you run the risk of basing your future decisions on unsubstantiated hypotheses. If you've been down that road before, you know it can be very dangerous, so make sure your findings can be qualified.

To get the desired validation you need, there are various routes you can take with varying degrees of time and cost attached. At the very least, we highly recommend speaking to your existing customers or speaking to prospects that you narrowly lost to a competitor, to gain insight. General engagement with your communities to see if you're on the right lines will also be beneficial to informing your inbound marketing strategy.

This type of validation can be an extremely valuable exercise to engage with your audience with a different agenda than usual and it's also a chance to demonstrate you're listening to, and you care about, your audiences' opinion.

Often we've seen this low-tech, low budget approach contributing significantly towards building brand loyalty; people are more likely to buy into a brand that they feel has listened and made decisions based on their opinion. Imagine if your favourite brands reached out to ask your opinion and changed the way they did things based on your feedback. How would you feel? Would you love them just a little bit more? So would we.

For a few more validation techniques, we also advise considering the following:

Industry market research
This can be expensive and longwinded, however, the more you know about the segments of your audience the better. You can often find a wealth of industry insights from websites like these:

tnsglobal.com
marketresearch.com
forrester.com
mintel.com
theinternettimemachine.com

You can access these, plus all of your resources for chapter three at:
ph-creative.com/Chapter3Resources

Solicited site feedback

Asking your audience for feedback on your website can be an incredibly powerful and insightful process.

However, it can be seen as intrusive and disruptive to your visitors and so it's not something you should undertake too often. If you do ask your website visitors for feedback you might want to think about offering some sort of incentive, to reward them for sharing their opinions.

Some useful feedback tools to consider include:

uservoice.com
polldaddy.com
usersnap.com
4QSurvey.com

You can access these, plus all of your resources for chapter three at:
ph-creative.com/Chapter3Resources

On-site search queries

Your search box can be a gold mine of information; from informing you what your audience is looking for on your website, to what particular language they're using to try and find it. If you control the sources of traffic coming into your different website pages, you can easily find insights relating to specific personas.

You should be using your search box database results to discover:

What people are struggling to find using your navigation menu (or other means)

What search queries return no results at all (this means you need to write more content)

What language is being used to describe your products and services

If you are correctly funneling your audience to relevant pages

Understanding your audience and mapping your personas is a vital stage in developing a robust inbound marketing strategy.

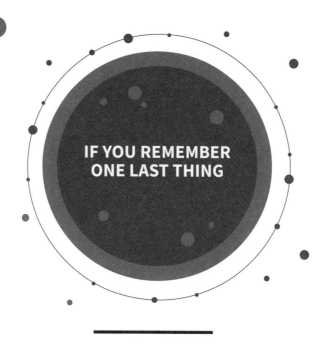

IF YOU REMEMBER
ONE LAST THING

Create content with your personas in mind.

Customers today expect authenticity, relevance and value from the brands they choose. Knowing exactly what your customers want and need from you means you're far more likely to engage with them on an emotional level.

If you don't understand what your audience truly wants, you might be getting goosebumps somewhere, but not from those who matter most – **your audience!**

Recommended reading & resources

BOOKS

Buyer Personas
Adele Revella
See your offering through your buyer's eyes for more effective marketing. Buyer Personas is the marketer's actionable guide to learning what your buyer wants and how they make decisions.

The New Rules of Marketing & PR
David Meerman Scott
Learn how to leverage the potential that digital communication offers your business by harnessing the power of the internet. Learn how to create compelling messages, get them in front of customers, and lead those customers into the buying process.

Peak
Chip Conley
Centring on Maslow's hierarchy of needs, Chip Conley walks readers through the process and strategy of building and sustaining a profitable business. Focusing on the experiences customers, employees and investors have with great companies, Peak explains how to inspire loyalty, brand status and ultimately foster maximum performance.

Persona and empathy mapping workbook download

Download our persona and empathy mapping workbook at the link below to start understanding your audience and begin mapping your personas.

ph-creative.com/Chapter3Resources

Takeaways for chapter 3

Ensure you've covered what's important and check off each stage below as you complete them.

☐ Map your persona profiles

☐ Understand their pain points and what they value

☐ Create content that appeals to their emotions and needs

RIGHT TIME RIGHT PLACE

An in depth look at where, when and what your audience spends their time looking at and who they are already influenced by.

"If we know what it was we were doing, it would not be called research, would it?"
Albert Einstein

"Research is formalised curiosity. It is poking and prying with a purpose."
Zora Neale Hurston

"If you're playing a poker game and you look around the table and you can't tell who the sucker is, it's you."
Paul Newman

With inbound marketing, it is not so much what you know, or who you know. It's more about what you know about who you don't know.

In today's digital world we now publish more content every 48 hours than all of the content ever published online up until 2004 combined. With figures like these in mind, it's safe to say that regardless of how micro your niche is, you have some competition.

As your marketplace becomes more crowded and your competition continues to get more difficult to beat, you need all of the marginal gains you can find to maximise the return on investment (ROI) of every piece of communication and content that you produce.

Simply producing great content that may be goosebump-worthy is sadly no longer enough to win in this game.

The strategy and effort behind your research and analysis is directly proportionate to the chances of your success online, so it's incredibly important – not a part of the process to be rushed or ignored.

This chapter focuses on three main areas to help you to get your content found more easily by your audience.

The first area of focus is the technical optimisation of your content in terms of both what your audience is looking for and how they are looking for it.

The second part of the chapter looks at how to find and engage with a relevant audience. Planning properly will help you generate visibility for the most appropriate content, within the context of what they're searching for.

Finally we look at how to find relevant influential people online (and offline) that can extend your reach and accelerate your exposure, through sharing and engaging with your content.

Optimising your content to be found online

Search Engine Optimisation (SEO) has been something of a moving target over the last ten years.

Ultimately, SEO has always stood for the process and discipline of manipulating the results of search engine rankings when a prospective customer is looking for your products and services online. The higher you rank, the more visible your site will be on search engines, thus leading to more traffic.

The ways and means by which you can achieve search engine visibility have changed drastically since the beginning of the practice and will continue to change as search engines continue to refine how they rank content.

There are over 200 factors that contribute to the ranking of each webpage found within Google. This ever-changing formula is continually refined to edge us closer towards mimicking the value a brand offers a customer in real life.

No longer are webpages listed in order of just relevance. Google now factors relevance, context and quality of experience delivered by a webpage into its rankings.

Social signals also play a role in deciding how credible and trustworthy a website is – if your website is receiving lots of socially-assisted traffic and links, search engines take this as a very positive sign.

"There are over 200 factors that contribute to the ranking of each webpage found within Google."

The business of
SEO is changing

The SEO industry is slowly admitting defeat from attempts to fool or out-manoeuvre Google; instead, SEO has become the art and science of playing by the rules.

Jamming keywords and phrases in the pages of your website that exactly match those typed into search engines by your audience is not only ineffective; it can be detrimental to the visibility of your website.

Instead of using what artificially pleases search engines to provide high visibility, you should place more emphasis on a strong user experience once a visitor lands on your website, pleasing both your customers and Google.

Google has made many changes to its algorithms to evolve the experience of search – aiming to reflect an experience you would find in the real world.

Panda — February 23, 2011
This major algorithm update hit sites hard, affecting up to 12% of search results (a number that came directly from Google). Panda cracked down on thin content, content farms, sites with high ad-to-content ratios and a number of other quality issues. This meant that websites set up solely for the purpose of

having links pointing to other websites (to seemingly manufacture popularity to boost rankings) were heavily penalised.

Venice — February 27, 2012
As part of their monthly update, Google mentioned code-name 'Venice'. This local update appeared to more aggressively localise organic results and more tightly integrate local search data. This update was designed to make it harder for a business to 'pretend' they were local to a particular area just by optimising for several local search words.

A good example of this would be a web agency in London using phrases such as 'web design Liverpool', just so they can generate business in Liverpool from afar.

Penguin — April 24, 2012
After weeks of speculation about an 'over-optimisation penalty', Google finally rolled out its 'Penguin' update designed to crack down on web spam. Penguin adjusted a number of spam factors, including keyword stuffing, and impacted an estimated 3.1% of queries in England.

Exact-Match Domain (EMD) Update — September 27, 2012

In 2012, Google announced a change in the way it was handling exact-match domains (EMDs). This led to large-scale devaluation of exact-match domains that were popular at the time.

Before this update, businesses realised that by using a domain which exactly matched keyword searches (for example, personalinjurysolicitorlondon.co.uk) they would rank well in Google just because of the domain name. Some businesses set up dozens of slightly different 'exact-match' domains to corner the market. This update burst their bubble and stopped ranking those websites highly in search results.

Hummingbird — August 20, 2013

Announced on September 26 2013, the Hummingbird update introduced changes to semantic search. In an attempt to provide highly relevant results Hummingbird focused on search context, rather than keywords. This update meant that you could be sure that your content would have more chance of being found by different people searching for the same content, but using slightly different language.

Mobile Responsive – April 21, 2015

Google's latest update marked a change to the ways in which it ranks websites, based on mobile responsivity. Whilst Google has been proactive in pushing the benefits of becoming mobile responsive, the latest update shows just how important it's become. This update changed the way that Google ranks – now based on usability – as mobile-first search grows in popularity.

SEO & audience personas

The world of technical SEO may be changing all the time; however your focus should remain on the experience of visitors, by providing an efficient service and great value through the content you produce and provide.

Good SEO means understanding a customer's intent to act and putting their needs first when devising and optimising the content you want them to consume. If your audience is new to your brand and not sure of the relevance or value of your offer yet, the hard or direct sell is inappropriate.

If, however, someone is familiar with your brand and wants to buy from you as quickly as possible, then a direct call to action is very appropriate. In both of these scenarios, it might be the same person but at different stages of their buying cycle. This means we need to think about different content for each stage of the buying cycle for each persona identified.

Gary Vaynerchuk sums this up:

"If content is king, context is God"

Optimising for just one set of keywords, or using the same language with all of your content is not the smartest way to approach inbound marketing.

The smart play is to use a blended approach, changing your language at each stage of the sales funnel to generate significant volumes of quality traffic. By taking such an approach, you will be more accurately assisting your customer's needs, as well as steering them further down your sales funnel.

We segment this sales funnel in the following way:

SEE, THINK, DO, DELIGHT

See, Think, Do, Delight

The basic premise of our philosophy is to use the insight you have gathered surrounding your various buyer personas to inform the content you present to them at each stage of a buying or engagement lifecycle. Put differently, we provide different types of content to the same buyer persona, depending on what they will most appreciate and value at the time.

By informing your content plan with this insight you can successfully move customers through an organised marketing funnel because you're considering the context of your audience's experience and recognising that the same audience will appreciate different types of content depending on their stage in the buying lifecycle.

The methodology of See, Think, Do, Delight clusters different types of content at each stage of the marketing funnel and tailors variations in language as a customer becomes more qualified as a lead (and the propensity to buy increases).

There are several different variations of the labelling of an inbound marketing funnel. HubSpot use their 'attract, convert, close, delight' model, which is largely similar to our own. In the interest of complete transparency, we've taken our wording from Avinash Kaushik, a well-known and respected author and digital marketing evangelist for Google. His blog can be found at kaushik.net and is well worth checking out.

Avinash uses this 'content context funnel' in a slightly different way to us – although his on-page technique is complementary to our methodology and should be embraced. Avinash uses SEE, THINK, DO to plan and order content that actually resides on a webpage. By his own admission, it is inspired by the good old AIDA model that copywriters have used to structure advertising copy since the late 1800s (attention, interest, desire, action).

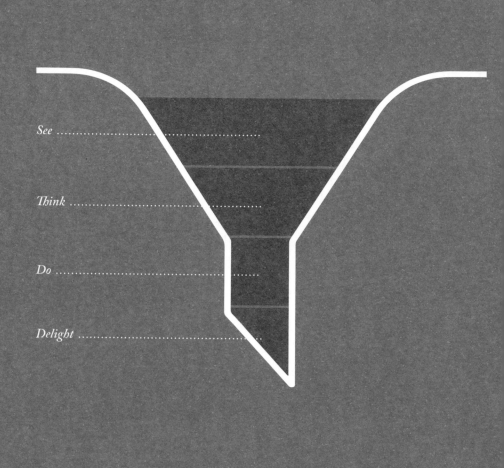

See ....

Think ....

Do ....

Delight ....

See

Objective:
To raise awareness. Activity at the 'See' stage consists of keywords, language and content that is designed to attract new, uninitiated 'strangers' at the start of the buying journey.

Think

Objective:
To position your business as a potential solution to your customers' challenge or problem. Activity at the 'Think' stage consists of keywords, language and content that is designed to provide material surrounding your brand and the specific, initial needs of your audience. This content adds value to the process by connecting the benefits of your offer with the intrinsic needs of the audience.

Do

Objective:
To facilitate a transaction of either contact details, insight into individual needs and/or unit sales. Activity at the 'Do' stage consists of keywords, language and content that is designed to convince a relatively qualified audience to take some form of action. This might not be moving in for an immediate sale, but it could be a download, a request for a call or more information.

Delight

Objective:
To maximise the life cycle of your customers and provide opportunities to refer more business. Activity at the 'Delight' stage consists of keywords, language and content that is designed to add value for existing customers or known prospects (through building trust, empathy and loyalty) in order to retain them and provide ongoing opportunities.

By understanding your audience at this granular level, you can integrate your content strategy with best practice SEO. You can maximise the reach of your content by using the right semantics and language throughout your inbound marketing.

Engaging with your audience on a more personal, tailored level at different stages of the marketing funnel means you can also communicate with a greater degree of accuracy and expect better results, by providing a better user experience.

Social media &
audience personas

Once you've defined who makes up your audience, you need to find out how they interact online. Social media is one of the easiest ways to gain valuable insight into your audience's interests and gauge their online habits.

Communities

Firstly, you need to find out where your audience lives online. Do they use specific social networking sites, or are they part of an online community? Are they influenced by anyone in the social sphere? If so, can you use these influencers to persuade and target them?

Hashtags

Just as important as knowing where your audience are going to be, you need to fully understand the kind of language they use on a daily basis. You should be researching what hashtags they frequently use and probing into how these hashtags reflect their interests.

Language can also be crucial in defining the intent of your audience. By analysing their conversations online you can define which stage in the buying cycle they're currently at – meaning you can tailor your messages to fit them personally. For example, if your research shows that your audience is often asking questions on social media, you should be optimising content which answers

their questions and pushing it through the platforms they frequent. If you're trying sell aggressively when your audience isn't ready, you'll fall flat.

Trend seasonality

Analysing how your customer's needs change and fluctuate throughout the year is also key to making sure your marketing is personalised and tailored for each customer. By undertaking effective keyword research and understanding hashtags and language, you can gauge exactly what your community is looking for and when.

Buying and browsing habits

By fully understanding the ways in which your audience shops, you can inform your strategy to fit with their needs. Understanding their habits can help you to turn a customer who has bought once, into a regular repeat customer. For example, if your customer is often buying bulk or family-sized products, you should be tailoring deals and offers to fit them.

Schema

Schema mark-up is additional tagging of content, within the code of a page, that provides a search engine with context surrounding your website's content. Schema mark-up helps a search engine contextualise your content, by making it easier to understand what your content is about. By using Schema mark-up, you are changing basic, generic information into structured data that can be organised and recognised by search engines. And that, in turn, makes it easier to match your content to search queries.

For example, if you wrap "StreetAddress" around '24 Queen Avenue', a search engine knows that '24 Queen Avenue' is an address. If you wrap "JobTitle" around the phrase 'Project Manager', a search engine knows that 'Project Manager' is a job role, and not the name of software, or a business principle.

Ultimately, the use of schema mark-up will help your website rank better and faster in search engine results pages than those that don't. So it's pretty much a no-brainer. For more information, visit schema.org, or try searching for 'Schema GTM', Google's Tag Manager.

schema.org

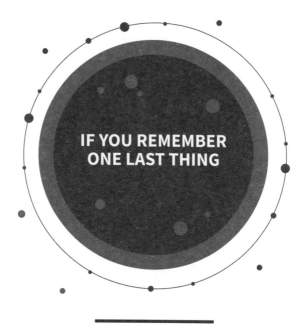

IF YOU REMEMBER ONE LAST THING

If you can provoke goosebumps with your content, you don't want it to be the best kept secret ever told.

However contagious your content is these days, getting your strategy right for reaching your audience and leveraging community influencers is key.

Follow our process and maximise your visibility within social channels and search engines too.

Recommended reading & resources

BOOKS

Word of Mouth Marketing
Idil M Cakim

Focusing on the traditional concept of word of mouth marketing, this book will help to identify online influencers, create stories that will resonate with your consumers and engage with influencers and customers online.

Webs of Influence: The Psychology of Online Persuasion
Nathalie Nahai

Online, everyone reacts differently to the websites, social channels and content they come into contact with. This book explores the psychology behind what makes people tick, in order to help you connect with customers, nurture relationships and create an online experience that attracts.

Inbound Marketing & SEO
Rand Fishkin & Thomas Høgenhaven

This book cherry picks the best and most popular inbound marketing articles from the Moz Blog – the go-to place for SEO and marketing insights – alongside some brand new essays. This book covers five channels of inbound marketing: content marketing, social media, outreach, conversion rate optimisation, and analytics, as well as search engine optimisation.

Become a Key Person of Influence
Daniel Priestley

Want to become an influencer in your field? This book outlines a specific five-step process to becoming a key person of influence within the inner circle of your industry – fast.

ONLINE TOOLS

SocialCrawlytics

An essential free tool in online research, SocialCrawlytics analyses URLs to establish how popular they have proved across the social space, this tool can also find influencers and work out how your competitors are doing. **socialcrawlytics.com**

Followerwonk

A nifty social media tool which allows users to search for keywords in Twitter users' biographies. Followerwonk is a fast and effective way to find your buyer personas' influencers (or just people who have the same interests as you). **followerwonk.com**

MentionMapp

Using data from the Twitter API, MentionMapp loads each user's Twitter updates, finds all of their interactions and hashtag mentions and displays them in a web-like format. MentionMapp makes researching your audience and influencers simple, allowing you to embark on a journey of discovery through a web of conversations and interactions.

mentionmapp.com

BuzzSumo

A great tool for finding influencers, BuzzSumo allows users to search for and filter influencers by their type. Influencer lists can be exported into an Excel file, which enables results to be filtered even further. The tool can also be used to find the most popular content around certain topics by searching a specific keyword and phrases.

buzzsumo.com

Nuzzel

Nuzzel is a useful tool for collating the stories and articles that have been shared by your friends on Facebook and Twitter. A social news aggregator, Nuzzel makes it simple to see what's important, without overwhelming you with data.

nuzzel.com

Twitter Advanced Search

The advanced search function within Twitter is one of the best and most under-utilised tools within the platform. Allowing you to specifically search for and target individuals based on particular keywords, phrases, locations and language, it makes identifying conversations and influencers within your field simple.

Understanding influencers download

Learn how to extend the reach of your content and seed effectively by getting to know the influencers in your field. Download your influencer ebook at the link below to get started.

ph-creative.com/Chapter4Resources

Understanding influencers download

Learn how to extend the reach of your content and seed effectively by getting to know the influencers in your field. Download your influencer ebook at the link below to get started.

ph-creative.com/Chapter4Resources

Takeaways for chapter 4

You should already have a solid set of audience personas mapped out, so by now you will be well and truly stuck into the research element of your inbound marketing strategy. Check off each step you complete below.

☐ Research what your audience are searching for online and their buying habits

☐ Plan your own sales funnel to map your buyer journey

☐ Understand their influencers

☐ Research some more

CHAPTER 5
HOW TO TELL A STORY

Master your ability to effectively communicate with impact and emotional intelligence in order to elicit the desired action.

"Effective communication is 20% what you know and 80% how you feel about what you know."
Jim Rohn

"People think in stories, not statistics, and marketers need to be master storytellers."
Arianna Huffington

"If history were taught in the form of stories, it would never be forgotten."
Rudyard Kipling

Storytelling could easily prove to be the true currency of modern day marketing.

The craft of shaping a story to ignite the imagination of your audience can be the difference between being remembered or instantly forgotten. Storytelling is massively undervalued by the vast majority of businesses when marketing themselves online.

As consumers or potential B2B customers we become numb to the masses of media messages we're forced to delete, or mentally skip to get to what we're looking for. We're fatigued, easily bored and distracted; ignoring the visual advertising on the screens we're simultaneously scanning. It's becoming harder to hold our attention.

If you're not aiming for goosebumps when telling your brand's story, then you're not reaching your full potential. You run the risk of wasting or under utilising all of the research, persona development and strategy planning you've undertaken so far. With enthralling stories you can leverage the power of storytelling and achieve remarkable results.

You may assume that you need an interesting subject in order to be regularly publishing contagious content. However, through the power of a compelling story, many businesses in perceived 'dull' industries have managed to create exciting, emotive content that keeps their audience engaged and coming back for more. Parisian Love by Google is the perfect example of a seemingly bland topic being made into a compelling piece of content through telling an emotional story.

In an advert that simply demonstrates the search engine process, Google tell a love story by using the myriad of search queries one man makes at important and memorable moments in his life. It works because we understand and relate to those moments. We've made many of those searches ourselves and we've been on that journey.

Check it out now by visiting the link below, before we look at the science behind this approach. **ph-creative.com/Chapter5Resources**

Google may only be selling their search platform, but they skillfully illustrate how their product adds value to real life situations.

If you're not convinced that Parisian Love is a particularly good example, we'd like to give you one more example to reinforce the idea that you don't have to be selling something sexy to be armed with what you need to tell an interesting story.

We've polled hundreds of people over the course of the year during conferences and keynote talks, to find out what the general consensus is with regards to the dullest sector or vertical market people can think of.

The overwhelming majority of those we have asked have agreed that insurance is considered the drabbest service you could ever possibly hope to find.

Who wants to hear about the provision of life insurance; about providing for your family in the event of a fatality? It's just not something you can dress up or easily make light of, right?

Well hold that thought…

Red Bull has carved an amazing niche for itself, strategically marketing in such a way that it appears to own the extreme sports world entirely. There's a good chance that most extreme sports videos will have its brand plastered all over them.

Red Bull has demonstrated its willingness to go to the ends of the earth to be crowned 'king of extreme sports' in everything it does. From masterminding stunts to extensive sponsorship of extreme sports, its brand exposure is unparalleled.

The story of Red Bull is a phenomenal one. We aren't claiming; 'if a sugar-fuelled soft drink can do it, anyone can'. That's not the point we're making here, because let's face it, soft drinks have always fared pretty well with marketing stories. Instead, the story of Red Bull should inspire all of us to set out a lofty strategic goal and work out exactly how to achieve it – no matter what it takes.

Now, imagine it wasn't Red Bull that set out that vision in the nineties, but instead an insurance company that specialised in life cover.

'No matter what life throws at you, we've got it covered.'

It could be argued that the Red Bull story would make just as much, if not more sense if it was being told by an insurance company. It could also be argued that if an insurance company was willing to be brave, they would have a much better chance of differentiating themselves from their competition.

Nigel Walsh, Vice President and Head of UK Insurance at Capgemini, highlights the importance of strong branding for insurers. As a leading figure in UK insurance, he understands the challenges faced by the industry when it comes to branding and marketing.

"The difference between insurance and many other industries is that we have an obligation to our customers for a mandatory product in a highly regulated world. We are not a throw away product or service. When people call us, it's usually in a state of duress due to an accident or emergency. It's all too easy to compare us on price comparison site and have no appreciation for our brand. That said, consumers and organisations absolutely have choice and the market is filled with great providers competing for your attention and money They can only do this by having the right product at the right price without compromising their ability to provide the service
expected when needed. To do this, they must have a brand you can and will trust."

Some insurance brands, however, are making a positive change in regards to the ways in which they market themselves. Proving that it's not always best to follow the herd, Hiscox Insurance stands out among its competitors for its clever use of marketing messages. Hiscox combines simplicity with compelling messages to relay its brand values and benefits. Its adverts engage with consumer pain points and ensure that the audience is aware that the brand understands and empathises with their experiences as small business owners. By doing this, it immediately creates rapport, trust and a sense of community within its demographic.

Whilst Hiscox is a great example of an insurance brand marketing itself well, there's still a long way to go if it wants to create goosebump-inducing results. To achieve these sorts of results yourself, you have to know your audience so well that you can predict, with a certain degree of accuracy, what their reaction will be.

You have to know what's important to your audience personas and what emotional drivers they will respond to. Incorporate this knowledge into a strong story and you too are ready to sell goosebumps.

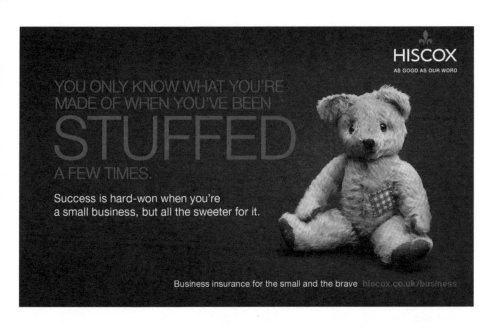

The science and
art of storytelling

Starting with a core reason to tell your story, then understanding how and when to tell it can transform your business.

Setting the scene

An old retired gentleman called Henry lived alone in Liverpool.

Henry didn't have much to occupy his time these days. He used to walk his dog, Scouse, each morning along a local beach before spending his afternoon at his allotment where he tended to his beloved vegetable patch, growing carrots, potatoes and his prize tomatoes.

Sadly, after Scouse passed away, Henry didn't go walking quite as much. When he did visit his allotment, it became ever more difficult to work the soil and look after his vegetables as he liked. His vegetable patch, once his pride and joy, had slowly become a site of frustration and upset.

Henry had a son, Vincent, an only child. Henry had loved nothing more than to take his young son to his allotment, bonding with him as they worked the soil, teaching him how to plant seeds and look after them as they grew.

Vincent was in prison now, after falling foul of peer-pressure and forces beyond Henry's control. Henry would write letters to his son, keeping him updated with his day-to-day life, and the progress of his allotment. This time, he described his predicament.

Dear Vincent,

I'm feeling pretty sad because it looks like I won't be able to plant the tomato garden this year. It's just getting too difficult for me now; I'm too old to be digging up a garden plot.

I know if you were here, you'd help me out, digging up the plot like years ago. I miss you son, stay out of trouble.

Love Dad.

A few days later, Henry received a letter back from his son.

Dear Dad,

Don't dig up the garden. That's where the bodies are buried.

Love Vincent.

At 4am the next morning, a team of local police and a small unit of special branch detectives arrived at the allotment and dug over the entire plot. Not a single body was found.

That same day Henry received another letter from Vincent.

Dear Dad,

Go ahead and plant your tomatoes now. That's the best I could do under the circumstances.

Love you, Vincent.

As well as being a heartwarming and funny story, the moral is that if you care enough, there's usually always something you can do for somebody else, no matter where you are.

This story also demonstrates how, as an audience, we can be drawn into a story and begin to empathise about a situation that's depicted well enough. What stories could you tell to provide your audience insight into your brand and start to become more approachable, personable and likeable? How can you begin to endear yourself to your audience and start to make your purpose something everyone can believe in?

If your audience began to feel the same sort of things for you and your brand as you did for Henry and Vincent you will experience something quite wonderful... you start to recruit fans instead of customers. You start to create something worth remembering and talking about.

First, **the science**

It is widely understood that all marketing decisions are emotional decisions. However, it is also important to recognise the need for rational thinking and logical information to reaffirm those emotional decisions.

A huge influence in the field of psychology and understanding the human mind is Dr. Steve Peters, author of The Chimp Paradox. Peters is a psychiatrist who has worked extensively with Great Britain's Olympic team and Liverpool Football Club. His insight into how the brain works and its reactions to stimuli has played a significant role in our approach to tailoring online marketing material.

With a greater understanding of how we think, we have a greater chance of stimulating our audience and maximising our chances of Getting Goosebumps.

Peters states that we have two sides to our brain. The first side of the brain is the emotional side, labelled the 'chimp'. The second side is the rational side, the 'human'.

To be truly effective when storytelling, both sides of the brain must be satisfied. Running through the following steps ensures the attention of both the 'chimp' and the 'human' are captured. Alongside Dr. Peters, there are many other psychology experts that talk about the distinct two sides of the brain and the importance of connecting with both sides to communicate effectively. Thinking, Fast and Slow by Daniel Kahnman is another book we would recommend reading on this subject.

From a marketing point of view, these psychological insights are key to crafting an informative and emotive story that helps us to showcase our products and services effectively.

We've learnt from extensive testing and measuring that satisfying both sides of the brain is essential to leading your audience through a story that successfully results in the action you want in the end. Stories should lead with emotion first and then satisfy the rational aspects of the thought process with facts, figures and evidence-based positioning.

"Creating authoritative content places you in front of people at the beginning of the decision making process."

Emotionally led thinking

Emotional drivers
There are five key emotions that drive the 'chimp':
happiness, sadness, fear, anger and anticipation.
When these emotions are evoked within us, we
seek to connect with others. This is the key to
spreading your business' message.

Speed
The 'chimp' brain reacts five times faster than any
other part of the brain, but what does this mean
for your digital reputation? If your webpage doesn't
load within three seconds, you could lose up to
40% of your online audience.

Empathy
The 'chimp' brain loves to connect. It wants to feel
that it is interacting with people who understand.
You have to know what your target audience is
talking about, and talk about it with them.

The pain and pleasure principle
The 'chimp' brain will do almost anything to avoid
pain. By understanding what the fears and pains
of your target consumers are, your brand can
provide them with a solution and capitalise on this
aversion to pain. Let your product or services be
their knight in shining armour.

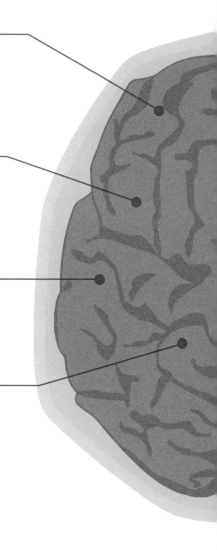

Evidence-based rational thinking

Facts and figures

The human part of the brain loves to make decisions based on cold hard facts. It wants social proof – such as user reviews and influencer recommendations – that what it is doing is right. Giving clear facts and sharing customer reviews is a great way to assure your customers about the experience they'll receive from your business.

Truth

If you're not truthful as an organisation, this reputation can spread from consumer to consumer. Genuine customer case studies will provide proof of your strengths as a business. If someone has a bad experience, acknowledgment can go a long way to recovering your reputation.

The bullshit monitor

The 'human' part of the brain has a well-developed critical function. People see over 10,000 links online every day and choose to ignore the majority of them. A convoluted and complicated sales message will get you nowhere fast. Simplify your message and deliver it with sincerity.

Thought leaders

Modern consumers research a product or service before they make the decision to buy. They look for justification that they're making the right decision. Creating authoritative content places you in front of people at the beginning of the decision making process.

A little more science

Pushing, pulling and guiding your audience in the direction you want to take them.

Smart Insights, a digital agency that focuses on providing advice and solutions to help businesses overcome their marketing challenges, has developed one of the most useful tools around to effectively plan your content. Their matrix system allows you to define your content and the thinking behind what you're trying to achieve when creating it. Thus, allowing you to effectively streamline your communications to be in-line with your brand values and your objectives.

Download your content matrix at the end of this chapter and in the meantime, check out what else they do at: smartinsights.com

Smart Insights advise that any marketing content you produce should evoke one of four

reactions. If you know your audience well enough and you know what you're trying to achieve, this matrix can help you select the right type of content to gain maximum effect.

You should be aiming to entertain, inspire, educate and convince with each piece of content you create for your brand.

Armed with this matrix, you can now craft purpose and context into your stories to make them truly effective. Content that follows these guidelines will assist your customer along their buying journey, moving them towards purchasing.

You will notice that some personas will respond to inspirational stories and messages at the beginning of their journey, while some will crave educational information. As always, the effectiveness of this process is determined by how well you know the personas of your audience.

And now, **the art**

When it comes to storytelling, marketers aren't even close to the top of the list of experts. If you want excellence, you should model yourself on the best.

We often find that looking outside of our profession is the best place to start.

Storytelling – learning from Hollywood

How does Hollywood remain so creative and continually tell different stories year after year? Well, it turns out they don't. There are really only six archetypal stories in Hollywood that get told and retold time and again. There is a tried and tested formula to these stories and it's rare for Hollywood to stray from this very profitable path.

The trick, of course, is to dress these stories up differently each time with different characters, challenges, scenarios and adventures.

However, the basic formula doesn't change.

Michael Hauge – author, lecturer and Hollywood script writer – outlines a step-by-step approach to storytelling. His method considers six basic stages, which are defined by five key turning points of all successful screenplays – a method which you can easily apply to any story you tell within your marketing.

Whatever industry you're in, understanding these key points and applying them to your stories will allow you to strengthen your ability to enthral your audience.

As well as following Hauge's steps to success, you should be looking for opportunities to add drama, add the unexpected and add a twist or to pique interest.

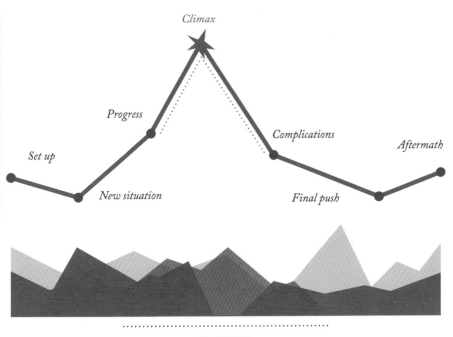

TENSION

DURATION

Michael Hauge's

Six stage plot structure

Below are six tangible points that translate well into a great technique for storytelling for business.

1. Be empathetic

Can you explain your message better from your audience's perspective? Hollywood scriptwriters make you live and breathe their story at every step. The empathy created helps your audience identify with the story and therefore, better engages them.

2. Make your customer the hero

Taking Hollywood as a prime example of storytelling to sell – they do one thing very, very well. They put you at the heart of the action and use 'reflection characters' to play alongside the hero. They serve to highlight certain characteristics in the main character and support them through their journey. But who is the hero in your story? It's not your brand or service – you're the reflection character. Your customer is the hero. Your product or service is simply the aid to solving their problem or issue.

3. Write for your audience

Use your knowledge about your customer's persona to write stories that resonate with them and appeal directly to their emotions. A great story could be lost on your audience if it isn't tailored to their needs, interests and desires.

4. Grab their attention straight away

Hollywood stories keep us hooked from the first couple of seconds – your stories need to do the same. In a world where attention-spans are short you need to make sure you grab your audience's attention from the off.

5. Hook them in and continue the story

Just as Hollywood movies tend to come in instalments, so too should your company's offerings to its customers. From the initial offer, the story must flow, each time providing an upgrade – you cannot be a one-hit wonder. If you want to survive online, you have to build a community and keep it alive.

6. Finally...

Every time you create a story, leave your audience wanting more. Your follow-up should not simply be expected, but anticipated. Try outlining a story based on one of your products or services using the Hollywood storytelling tricks above. Remember your customer should always be the hero in your story, your product or service should be the solution to their problem. Try using the one of the customer personas that you created in chapter three as the central character in your story. Remember to think about pathos, ethos and logos and how these can combine to create goosebumps. Fill out the stages on the next page or download your own printable version by visiting **ph-creative.com/Chapter5Resources**

"Who is the hero in
your story?"

Setup:

Explain a typical situation that a customer might find himself or herself in. This stage must draw your audience in and allow them to identify with the hero of your story.

Die Hard:

John McClane is returning home to his family for Christmas.

_____

_____

_____

New situation:

Describe a set of circumstances that see the situation change and create a potential introduction for your product or service or perhaps a competitor.

Die Hard:

John McClane and his wife are attending a Christmas party, however, the building has been over taken by Hans Gruber and a team of terrorists.

_____

_____

_____

Progress with the new situation:

Here your hero's journey should be going to plan and all obstacles should be easily overcome. Use this as a chance to craft emotion into your story and connect your audience to your brand.

Die Hard:

The terrorists storm the building, but McClane isn't in the room. This means he is able to move up the building with little hindrance.

_____

_____

_____

Complications and higher stakes:
Introduce a plot twist, or an unexpected change to the plan at this point. Consider a surprise element and create a situation that looks almost incomprehensible.

Die Hard:
The police send in a SWAT team to tackle the terrorists, but the team fails.

_____

_____

_____

Final push:
This is where all is seemingly lost but there's one final, slim chance to save the situation. This could be subtle, dramatic or it could be emotional.

Die Hard:
After a struggle, John McClane throws Gruber out of a high floor window, resulting in his death.

_____

_____

_____

Aftermath:
The aftermath stage will see your hero's life return to normality once again, albeit with some differences and key benefits now that your hero has come so far.

Die Hard:
Normality is restored when the police release the hostages from the building. The McClanes leave in a police car and return to their lives.

_____

_____

_____

Storytelling
– learning from great leaders

Many great leaders are defined by the great speeches they have delivered. JFK, Martin Luther King and Winston Churchill are just a few who have been immortalised by their words.

As business leaders and marketers, you may not be fighting for world peace or global cultural change; however, you are fighting for your cause and what your brand stands for. It is therefore your job to communicate the facts and provide a rationale to appeal to the human side of the brain. However, it is the sentiment behind the message that captures the chimp's imagination and gives your audience goosebumps.

Here's the top six ways we can embrace teachings from great leaders:

1. Start with the context
If you don't start your story with the fundamental context, you'll lose your customer from the beginning. Don't assume they always know what you're talking about. Don't waffle, but do make sure you set the scene.

2. Be passionate
Does your message show how you really feel? Some of the greatest leaders in history are memorable and iconic because of their passion. Martin Luther King said, 'I have a dream' not 'I have a three-point-plan' for a reason.

3. Make sure emotion makes it into your message
If you want to evoke an emotional response from your customers, you need to make sure you script that emotion into your message. If your message isn't powerful to begin with, your response won't be either.

4. Use your own experiences
Some of the most powerful leaders use factual evidence in their speeches to tap into the emotions of their audience. Illustrations of struggle, failure, and barriers are what make leaders appear authentic and accessible. Your story should do the same.

5. Keep it simple

Just as you would revisit content and remove unimportant details, you should do the same with your storytelling. Remove anything that isn't central to your message, leaving just a few well-placed interesting details which will help your audience relate.

6. Finally...

Story is the fabric upon which culture is built. We tell stories every day of our lives – they bind us together, help us form relationships and ultimately, can drive change. Remember how powerful a story can be and make sure yours meet all of the markers you set out in the beginning.

History reimagined

Can you imagine if some of the most famous and recognisable speeches in history had been written without the passion for which they have become renowned? Take a look below at Winston Churchill's 'We shall fight on the beaches' speech during the Second World War. It's one of the most quoted and analysed speeches in British history.

"We shall go on to the end. We shall fight in France, we shall fight on the seas and oceans, we shall fight with growing confidence and growing strength in the air, we shall defend our island, whatever the cost may be. We shall fight on the beaches, we shall fight on the landing grounds, we shall fight in the fields and in the streets, we shall fight in the hills; we shall never surrender..."

Winston Churchill, June 4th 1940

Now imagine if this speech had been written using the business jargon often employed in the corporate world:

"Going forward, we will experience conflict in many arenas. We shall infiltrate the French demographic and with growing confidence we can leverage our offering in this space and maximise the impact of our presence in the vertical market, whatever the average spend may be. We shall step up to the plate on every level. We shall hustle until close of play."

See, when it's lacking the passion and sentiment to capture the chimp's attention it fails to resonate.

"...therefore your job is
facts and provide a ratio
human side of the brain
sentiment behind the n
the chimp's imagination
goosebumps."

o communicate the
ale to appeal to the
However, it is the
ssage that captures
nd gives your audience

Storytelling
– learning from comedians

Stand-up comedy has got to be one of the toughest careers there is. Imagine standing alone in front of a live audience with nothing but a microphone and collection of stories, anecdotes and one liners designed to make a room full of strangers laugh out loud.

Jerry Seinfeld noted that good comedy has a way of sticking with you and finding a way to keep coming back, but how can you use this logic to create a story that people will remember?

Here's the top five recommendations to think about:

1. Write about what you know

When creating content you should pick a topic, which you know inside out. Make sure you can attack it from every angle. It's far better to write with confidence about a subject you know well than one you don't.

2. Build it up

How many comedians do you know that start with a punchline? Comedians will set the scene by painting a picture and making their topic relatable. It's important you do this too, because you need to assess why your customer should care about your content.

If you can't provide a compelling story, which naturally builds to a punchline, you're going to fall flat. It's also worth noting that many of the best comedians all agree that the punch line word needs to come right at the end of that last sentence to make the biggest impact.

3. Be memorable

What clear takeaway should your customer receive from your story? Make it obvious exactly what it is you want them to remember, even if it means you have to mention it more than once.

4. Tie everything together

Comedians often use a technique called a call-back to tie everything together. They will revisit the same punchline at the beginning and end of their set, to build intimacy and make their audience feel like they're part of an inside joke.

You should be doing the same when creating compelling stories – always tie up your story with a resolution to every problem you introduce.

To connect with your audience, you first must be able to deliver a message that's easy to understand and remain memorable once it's been delivered.

One rule many leaders and comedians use is the rule of three. Hollywood screenplays are written in three act structures and even great lawyers argue three points at a time.

5. Be compelling

People don't invest in your business; they invest in your story. If you want people to remember what you say, tell a compelling story. Give people something they can't wait to share.

So you can see, marketers can learn a lot from other professional communicators. But what else is it that all of these have in common?

The Rule of Three

For some reason, things just work better in threes.

The rule of three is a writing principle that suggests things that come in threes are funnier, more satisfying and easier to understand (did you see what I did there?).

Some say there's a psychological reason based on 'three' being a pattern that's easier for the audience to digest and remember. Others say it's just the way it goes. The art of writing a good joke can be broken down in to these three parts and you can use the exact same technique to craft a wining marketing message.

In films
1. Sex, Lies and Videotape
2. The Three Musketeers
3. The Good, The Bad and The Ugly

In leadership
1. Friends, Romans, countrymen
2. There are three kinds of lies: lies, damn lies and statistics
3. I came, I saw, I conquered

In advertising
1. Beanz Meanz Heinz
2. Snap! Crackle! Pop!
3. Just do it

The rule of three is prevalent in all forms of effective communication but is most commonly associated with comedy writing because it works and it works very well. How can you use the rule of three in your marketing to get goosebumps from your audience? Why not start by taking some inspiration from comedy and an even greater example of the rule of three in action?

The classic structure of a joke: The setup, The anticipation, The punchline

The setup
A woman gets on a bus with her baby. The bus driver says: 'Ugh, that's the ugliest baby I've ever seen!'

The anticipation
The woman walks to the rear of the bus and sits down, fuming. She says to a man next to her: 'The driver just insulted me!'

The punchline
The man says: 'You go up there and tell him off. Go on, I'll hold your monkey for you.'

The setup
I went to the zoo the other day.

The anticipation
There was only one dog in the whole place.

The punchline
It was a Shitzu.

Try breaking down your favourite joke in to the rule of three, or better yet, try to write your own joke! Fill out the steps on the next page or download your own printable version at
ph-creative.com/Chapter5Resources

The setup:

The anticipation:

The punchline:

Now try to write a short anecdote using this form of phrasing. Don't worry too much if it's not side splittingly funny, just concentrate on crafting the flow of the message.

A good example of this can be seen in Pepsi's Uncle Drew campaign.

Watch it by visiting your chapter 5 resources page and then try to create your own using the same principles.

The setup: Set the scene.
Uncle Drew:
Pepsi pretends to shoot a documentary on a basketball player named Kevin at a local outdoor court, where he's playing with friends. Kevin's Uncle Drew comes along to watch the game.

The anticipation: Present a relevant situation.
Uncle Drew:
A team player injures himself, presenting the opportunity for elderly Uncle Drew to join the team. After a shaky start, he's netting balls swiftly and showing up the entire team.

The punchline: Surprise with an unexpected benefit.
Uncle Drew:
Uncle Drew defies belief with his skills – until he is revealed to be Gary Ervin, a professional American basketball player.

Experience mapping
and design

Feel
Think
Ease
Memory

Most brands invest significant time and
resource designing messaging and positioning
their brand with their audience, however very
few invest in designing what it feels like to
experience a brand.

If the messages are slick but the service is
poor, how do you judge a brand?

If the story is inspiring but the reality is
disappointing, how do you judge a brand?

Audience experience
– a unique model

It's crucial to remember that every audience touch point that you create matters to your brand. You're being judged at every stage and you're only as strong as your weakest link. At Ph.Creative we implement the model Feel, Think, Ease and Memory.

Each key element of our carefully crafted model is designed to ensure that your audience moves consistently further along a set process — finishing their journey with a positive and lasting memory of your brand.

Important considerations
It's essential you ask yourself these crucial questions:

What is the purpose of the event?

Where must the event take place?

What is the most important focal point of the event/scene?

What one sentence sums up this scene?

Finish this sentence: 'In this scene, the audience must...'

Finish this sentence: 'In this scene, we must...'

What are the success criteria of the event?

What are the potential risks to the event?

What technology is being used?

What information must be captured?

What else must be achieved during this event?

What are the steps involved?

Who is involved in this event? What is their role/purpose?

Feel

In order to understand how candidates are feeling every step of the way, you must first truly understand who they are. This requires more than their basic details. It's each of their needs — all of their ambitions. It's their personalities and above all else what makes them tick. Each piece of information you can gather will equip you with the insight to devise an audience experience that truly works.

Always ask yourself:
What emotions are they feeling?
How strongly do they feel about it? (from 1 to 10)

Think

It's time to get inside candidate's heads. What exactly are they thinking? If you're placing yourself in their shoes, they should never be left to chase up feedback themselves. It's in your own interest as a brand to follow up after an interview. Show that you care about their opinion. Send out a survey or simply ask for some feedback on the process so far. You need to know what your candidates are thinking wherever possible.

Always ask yourself:
What are they thinking?
What is the importance of this opinion?
(from 1 to 10)

Ease

How smoothly does your audience experience run? It's hugely important to realise that a slow and tedious application system will lose your brand some of the best potential talent. Take your process for a test drive yourself. If you find it long and complicated, the chances are that your candidates will too. Consider your unsuccessful candidates too — they're far more likely to reapply in future if they found the process simple. Your 'candidate experience' factor determines the calibre of your candidates and the reputation associated with your brand.

Always ask yourself:
How easy is the experience for the candidate?

Memory

Don't let unsuccessful candidates fall into the abyss. A successful audience experience will be memorable for all the right reasons. Your focus should be to inspire rather than dishearten your candidates — even the ones who don't get the news they want at the end of the process. Ensure that they see value in the overall interaction with your brand. After all, when they spread the word, you want them to say something positive.

Always ask yourself:
How memorable is the overall experience?
(from 1 to 10)
What is the most memorable moment and why? (from 1 to 10)

Purpose

Consider the purpose of every stage of your candidate journey. Closely monitor whether sections of the experience feel unnecessary. If they don't appear to resonate with the candidate, or simply fail to push the candidate towards the next part of the journey, it's time to remove them from the process altogether.

It's far better to eliminate that section of the journey early on, rather than risk ideal candidates dropping because they found it tedious.

People/stakeholders

Stakeholders include the people who become involved in your candidate's journey. This includes anyone from managers and directors to external recruiters.

No matter who is telling your brand story, your vision and values should remain precise and consistent. For example, when external recruiters are involved, their perception of your brand should align with the story told by your internal employees.

Technology

Technology can be a game changer for your recruitment process, pushing you ahead of competitors in the long run.

For example, the software we began devising while working with Virgin Media aims to measure the happiness of candidates as they complete their journey, while also offering all applicants valuable insight that will strengthen their employability. The overall aim is to leave them feeling positive about the brand, whatever the outcome.

Experience validation

Always remember that you can't be sure that your audience experience is right for your candidates without testing the waters first for yourself.

Invest time in using the following techniques to validate your audience experience:

Surveying customers and team members

Frequent public polls

Desk research — including media, journalists, published reports, universities

Pilot observations

IF YOU REMEMBER
ONE LAST THING

Make sure you know who your customer is
and make them the hero in your story by
showing them how you make their life easier.

Ensure you script emotion into your message and
create a story so compelling your audience is left
with goosebumps.

Recommended reading & resources

BOOKS

Contagious
Jonah Berger
This book teaches us that people don't share information – they share stories that resonate with them emotionally, which just so happen to include information about a product or service.

Pitch Anything
Oren Klaff
This book shares the secret to closing any business deal. It introduces the STRONG method of pitching, a method which is as relevant online as it is in the boardroom:

- Set the frame
- Tell the story
- Reveal the intrigue
- Offer the prize
- Nail the hook point
- Get a decision

Resonate
Nancy Duarte
Revealing the truth behind creating impactful and inspiring presentations that move your audience into purposeful action, Resonate helps you make a connection with your audience through exciting, fun and meaningful presentations. Using this approach, you'll convey your content with passion, persuasion, and impact.

Talk Like TED
Carmine Gallo
TED and associated TedX conferences are held in more than 130 countries and are viewed at a rate of 1.5 million times a day. Want to give your own presentations this edge? This book breaks down the fundamental principles used in the top TED talks so that you can use these tips yourself and create dynamic, successful presentations.

Clout: The Art and Science of Influential Web Content
Colleen Jones
This book explains the importance behind using influence to gain traction within your online strategy. Through outlining the eight principles of influence, Clout covers all bases, from context, to the art of rhetoric, to the science behind customer psychology.

Create your own content matrix download

Download our guide to creating your own content matrix by visiting your resources page for this chapter. This will help you to start planning the types of content you can create for every stage of your strategy.

ph-creative.com/Chapter5Resources

Takeaways for chapter 5

You should now understand the importance of a well thought out story and the impact thiscan have on all of your marketing messages. You should also be starting to incorporate the professional tactics we discuss into your storytelling methods. Check off each step you complete below.

☐ Incorporate your persona research when creating your story

☐ Plan your story, mapping what each persona needs from you at each point of their journey

☐ Script emotion into your messages and storytelling

☐ Plan your storytelling like the professionals, using our step-by-step guides

THE STORY SO FAR

How all of the previous components and ideas fit together into one neat plan you can work from and rely on.

"Get shit done."
Aaron Levie

"If you can't explain it simply, you don't understand it enough."
Albert Einstein

"However beautiful the strategy, you should occasionally look at the results."
Winston Churchill

It's time to find out if everything we've looked at has merely been fun and interesting, or whether it's actually making sense and could be of value to your business. Hold tight.

Most of our strategic marketing thinking at Ph. is represented, in some way shape or form, in our content planning spreadsheet. You can download your own version at **ph-creative.com/Chapter6Resources**

We know it's a big ask to expect a marketer to go away, download a spreadsheet and get a little excited about what they find. Hopefully, a lot of what we've explored so far will make sense to you at first glance and you start to find value in what you see.

The simple version of the spreadsheet is included here because the principle behind its creation ought to be the primary message. In the next chapter, we've included a detailed content calendar to help you plan your activities on a daily basis and tailor your content to meet your overarching business objectives in a more detailed format.

If you don't immediately see the value of the spreadsheet, have a go at filling it in anyway. We think it's likely to have one of three effects on the way you view your digital marketing:

- The inbound (content) marketing penny will drop and you'll see a direct link between producing content for your audience and achieving your strategic business goals

- You'll recognise the value of the format and you can immediately get going with planning your strategy

- You'll recognise that someone else in the business will find lots of value using the document and now inbound marketing makes sense to you

How to get the most out of this document

Start with Tab 1 – marked 'Content Calendar'.

With this document you will be able to define your goals and plan the next six months' worth of marketing activities in line with your target personas.

Fill in zone one – business objectives

Take your overarching business purpose, as established in chapter 1, and place it in the first box. Follow this by stating your key business objectives for the next two quarters in each of the numbered spaces, and add three content themes for each quarter. For example, your content themes could be focused on specific elements that are important within your field or sector.

Fill in zone two – monthly performance indicators

Now you know what you want to achieve, make it tangible and black and white by assigning a numerical value that determines what success looks like for each month.

From our own experience, 99% of marketers do not set out tangible goals or set a benchmark for success when planning their digital marketing activities. Of the 1% that do, less than half can show a clear correlation between their digital marketing goals and that of the overall businesses objectives.

Whatever happens from here, by using this spreadsheet you will know what you're gunning for and so will your team.

Fill in zone three – persona keyword sets

Define what keywords you will be using to target your personas based on your research from chapter 3. This spreadsheet has room for three personas: if you've identified more, it's best to create an additional document for the others.

When filling this section in, it's important you identify key characteristics of each persona at the different stages of the **SEE, THINK, DO, DELIGHT** funnel and match your keywords accordingly.

SEE - What messages are likely to get their attention at the top?

THINK - What benefits and messages are likely to resonate with them once they're aware of you?

DO - What is likely to be the most attractive and effective call to action for this persona?

DELIGHT - What added value will each persona appreciate and respond to after they have bought from you for the first time?

Fill in zone four – content plan

Using the picture you have built up of each audience persona, earmark the type of content you believe to be most suitable at each stage. Use the principles of the Smart Insights matrix in chapter 5 to decide what type of content to use, but don't worry just yet about what the story is going to be – that comes next. For now, you're merely trying to gauge what your audience will be most likely to respond to.

Also, bear in mind the amount of time/budget you have to spend on each persona in each month. This will be a very useful means of pacing and budgeting your marketing

efforts. Keep an eye on the success criteria you've already determined in ZONE TWO because the effort needs to match the desired outcomes – does it pass the litmus test?

Now is a very good time to decide how many personas you're going to actively engage with month by month. You should be able to identify 'core' content that will supplement any specific persona-targeted content – is there enough content to achieve success?

Move to tab two/zone five – influencer research

Using the keyword and influencer research techniques covered in chapter 4, complete the fields in this tab. There are three tabs, one for each persona. Remember the language and keywords you define will become more specific, targeted and long tail (a long tail keyword is a search string with usually more than three specific keywords included) the further into the buying cycle you go.

Get **creative**

There's no zone to be filled out here. Instead, you need to begin writing a brief for the specific types of content you've identified in zone four. Begin to brainstorm the specifics of your content using the storytelling inspiration from chapter 5. This is the toughest, most challenging aspect of inbound marketing.

Creating truly effective, valuable content for your audience is the make or break point of this entire marketing philosophy. One final bit of advice here is to be prepared to fail with content more than you succeed. And remember, you learn just as much from what doesn't work as what does.

Implement your plan with winning tactics

From your research into where your audience lives online and how and what they are likely to respond to, now comes the most interesting aspect of the whole process. This is the bit where you take a deep breath and actually start doing it. Publish, listen, respond and refine – with the tactics you decide are most relevant.

The final step – measure, refine, learn, repeat. Measure, refine, learn, repeat.

Measure, Refine, Learn, Repeat.

There's not a whole lot more to add to the title of this step. Just go for it.

One key element to your success, however, is using the right tools for the job.

Ph.Creative is a HubSpot partner (full disclosure) and we passionately believe our customers have an advantage in their marketplace because of the intelligence we have at our fingertips. The speed at which we can move and respond, based on what we learn by using this tool, allows us to measure and interpret results in a much more meaningful and, ultimately, strategic way.

Your strategy should be guided based on cause and effect. Evidence based marketing is the only game you should be playing. Consider using a content marketing tool such as HubSpot.

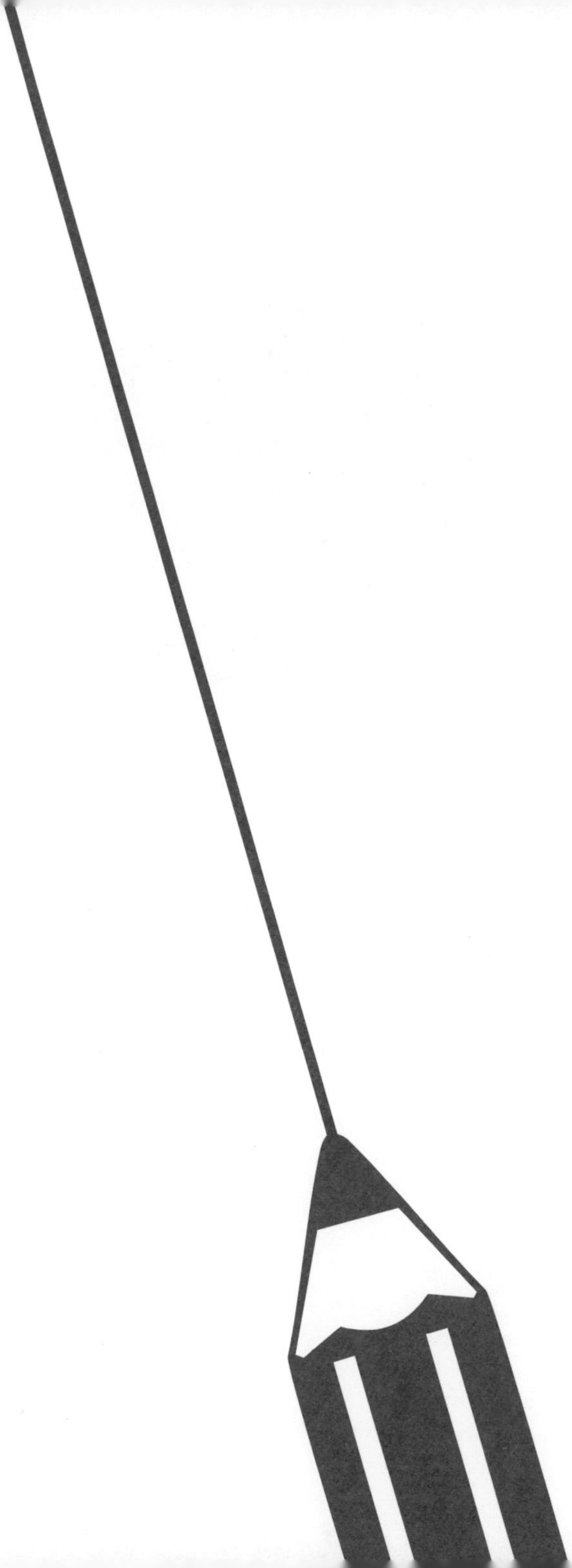

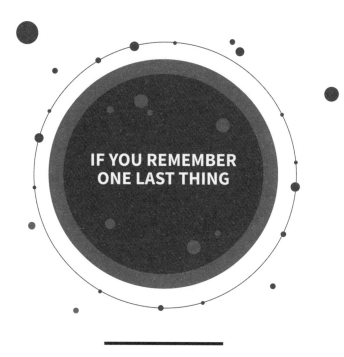

IF YOU REMEMBER ONE LAST THING

By now you're nearly ready to unleash your own brand of goosebumps on the world. It's got to be efficient, effective and, above all, aligned to your business objectives.

This process can be as simple or as detailed as your plan dictates but it's got to add value to your business. This chapter is here to ensure you do just that.

Recommended reading & resources

BOOKS

Inbound Marketing – Attract Engage and Delight Customers Online
Brian Halligan & Dharmesh Shah

Written by CEO and Founder of HubSpot, Brian Halligan, and CTO and Founder Dharmesh Shah, this book details how businesses can embrace inbound marketing through the latest insights and advice for lead nurturing. The book addresses how to best convert visitors and how to continue to delight them after they've passed through your sales funnel.

Search & Social: Rob Garner

A must–read for anyone in the digital marketing sector, this book shows you how to develop, implement and optimise strategies and tactics to develop your strategic marketing plan.

Content planning strategy spreadsheet download

Download our content strategy planning template by visiting the link below for use alongside this chapter. Start making your marketing more successful by aligning your objectives, goals and content, coupled with full influencer research to help maximise your reach.

Fill out the steps below, or download your own printable version at

ph-creative.com/Chapter6Resources

Key takeaways for chapter 6

It's now time to start putting everything we've talked about into place and start creating your successful inbound marketing strategy. Download our spreadsheet (if you haven't already) and check off each step as you complete it.

☐ Download the spreadsheet and fill it in using your research

☐ Put your plan into practice

☐ Review how your plan is performing at regular intervals

CHAPTER 7: part 1
THE MASTER PLAN

A comprehensive look at the skills you need to action your plan.

"Do you want to know who you are? Don't ask. Act! Action will delineate and define you."
Thomas Jefferson

"Everyone has a plan until they get punched in the mouth."
Mike Tyson

"Productivity is never an accident. It's always the result of a commitment to excellence, intelligent planning and focused effort."
Paul J Meyer

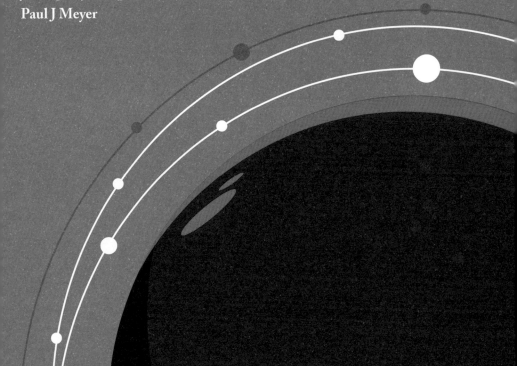

"The number of times we hear, 'social media doesn't work for me' is unbelievable."

A digital strategy is a lot like a car tyre: without sufficient traction, you don't go anywhere. All too often we see businesses working hard and producing great content, yet they fail to get the traction they need to move forward.

In this chapter, we explore how to choose the right tools and channels for your strategy. We will also outline some fundamental tactics to help you leverage marginal gains and drive your inbound marketing forward.

Ultimately, there's only one way you're going to find out what works for your audience, your business and your objectives – that's by doing it. Testing, reacting and committing enough to do it well, even when it's not going as well or as fast as you would like.

The number of times we hear, 'social media doesn't work for me' is unbelievable. If you've ever said that yourself, we can assure you that it's you not working for social media, not the other way around. But you're not alone, so don't worry. Inbound marketing is easy with the right approach, but it's hard work. If you love the idea of Getting Goosebumps it's probably a good idea to start loving the idea of hard work and a commitment to excellence.

A final point before we jump into it. Goosebumps can't happen every time you publish content – it's just not possible. You can, however, stack the odds in your favour by following the rules laid out in this book.

Use this book to guide your approach; as a proven playbook that's delivered success many times over. It's not a 100% bullet proof process for your content to fly each and every time. However, this is not all bad. Having content sink now and then is a very good opportunity to engage with your audience.

Too many marketing teams fail with content and move on quickly to new ideas, missing opportunities. Sometimes, making a small tweak to content that has failed means you'll find it does well second, third or fourth time around.

All great marketers have produced content that has failed the first time around, but through asking their community for ways to improve, it's been successfully re-launched. Some of this content even continues to drive traffic years later.

Getting organised for day-to-day

Whether you've flicked straight to this chapter or you're reading this book from start to finish, by now you should be comfortable with the strategic direction of your inbound marketing. At this point you need to be ready to get down to the nuts and bolts of day-to-day implementation.

The previous chapter's download provides a succinct means of mapping the activity required to deliver your desired goals each quarter. However, it does not provide the help you need in planning your day-to-day actions or with managing time, researching, producing and seeding out your content.

To combat this, download our template content calendar, which will provide a clear framework in which to organise everything you need going forward. You'll find this in your chapter 7 resources page.
ph-creative.com/Chapter7Resources

This document will help you to map daily content tasks and also determine the most appropriate destination in which to publish. That means which social channels your content is designed for and which persona it's being targeted at as well.

Keeping a track of your week-to-week progress is the key to maintaining a consistent and professional inbound marketing plan. This is especially true when there's more than one person involved in the delivery and seeding of your content. With this in mind, we highly recommend using the 'owner' and 'completion date' fields to ensure everything is completed as and when required.

This document is very basic and designed to illustrate this approach. There are more advanced tools available online to manage team productivity and tasks; however this simple spreadsheet provides a great start.

Leveraging influencers and opportunities

Effective social media use is similar to networking in a room full of people that find your message relevant and interesting; on that we can probably all agree. We can also agree that the fastest way to see decent results is by talking to the people who a) know what they're talking about and b) already hold the attention of the others in the room.

Building a following online is just like rubbing shoulders with people who matter in the real world to get ahead. Social status counts for everything. When you talk, you want people to listen, share and engage with you. If the people you're engaging with already have an audience or following, you're headed in the right direction.

It's not just what you know and it's not just who you know. It's now also about what you know about who you know... and how you maximise that knowledge.

Leveraging other people's influence: ego-jacking

Dale Carnegie's *How to Win Friends and Influence People* is still as relevant today as it was when it was first written in 1936; driven by the principle:

"You can make more friends in two months by becoming interested in other people than you can in two years by trying to get other people interested in you."

Ego-jacking is the art of putting someone in the spotlight and making them look brilliant for what they've achieved and accomplished. The name of the game is to flatter your target influencers. This way, they will acknowledge your existence socially, exposing you to their extended network.

This can be a blunt instrument if not handled with care. Your content must pass the bullshit test. If you're obviously blowing smoke up the ass of people you'd like to make friends with, it can backfire very quickly. The golden rule is to make sure you're accurate and fair with praise – give credit where it's due, not where it's convenient.

Some devices to consider when ego-jacking:

Infographics

The advantage of using infographics is the ease with which they can be scanned and understood at a glance. Quite often, an infographic will be used to explain a process, timeline of events or anything that can be easily illustrated in a visual way. Infographics can also be extremely effective at explaining a concept or even a pretty technical subject quickly and easily.

One particularly effective use of an infographic for ego-jacking purposes is to map influencers together with a particular subject to highlight their contribution, or how a sequence of events, theories and thoughts have developed over time.

Whilst being extremely interesting and valuable to the corresponding niche audience, the infographic is particularly appealing to the influencers themselves. Can you imagine seeing your name included within someone else's marketing, giving you credit and holding you in high regard, for all to see?

Whether your infographic blatantly maps people or a process or something completely different, the key is to give credit to the influencer. If you include a link back to the influencer's profile or website, there's more reason for them to share it once you've got their attention.

You'll find some examples that we love at **ph-creative.com/Chapter7Resources**

Listicles

A listicle does what is says on the tin. It's a list of things or people – usually illustrating the 'top 100' or the 'best 25' etc. These lists tend to be sharable and desirable to people with an interest in that particular niche. After all, you're saving them the time it would take to do the research themselves. Obviously, when your name is listed amongst the ranks, you would be likely to share it too.

Listicles can be one of the most blatant ego-jacking tools, so try this approach with caution. If it's too similar to other lists, if it's pretty obvious and doesn't offer any new insight, some influencers will regard it as too repetitive to share. However, it can also be the most effective way to drive results, if done well. The key is coming up with a new angle which presents a fresh way to boost their egos. If it's not particularly time sensitive, you could find it contributes a decent level of traffic consistently for quite some time.

You'll find some examples that we love at **ph-creative.com/Chapter7Resources**

Infographics

Reviews

Listicles

Interviews

Reviews

A great way to demonstrate knowledge or expertise is to give your opinion with some interesting insight that will be of use to your audience. A handy by-product of this is showcasing the value of an influencer's intellectual property, such as a book, white paper or webinar. You can easily find yourself being promoted by the influencer as a result.

Interviews

Short of co-authoring a book or creating some sort of collaboration, interviewing your influencers is the next best thing you can do to maximise exposure to their network.

The trick to taking full advantage of an interview opportunity with an influencer is to ask great questions and allow the influencer to answer in a way that showcases their best stories, achievements or key points they're looking to highlight.

Be sure to ask timeless questions so the content isn't immediately out of date. Consider asking your audience for questions and suggestions before the interview so you can build engagement even before the interview takes place.

Interviews also provide you with a great opportunity to learn from experts and influencers to better inform your own goals and objectives.

Leveraging the news: news-jacking

Being relevant is one of the biggest success factors in inbound marketing. If you're not relevant, you're not important or useful to anyone and you're not going to get very far.

You should be monitoring your community closely and engaging on topical issues as they happen. The easiest way to do this is to set up a number of news alerts; Google Alerts work well for this. From here, work out a simple daily or weekly routine consisting of key websites to monitor – either by visiting them or by subscribing to their RSS feeds to receive latest updates.

By producing stats or information that nobody else has currently been able to, or by having an alternative or interesting spin on something topical, you will be able to successfully differentiate yourself from the noise. The trick is to ride the wave as it breaks and propel yourself into the mix of conversation as it unfolds.

Follow these five simple rules and you'll do just that!

1. Be flexible
Opportunities don't always look like the ideas in your plans.

2. Be nimble
Effective news-jacking requires acting fast.

3. Be open-minded
Explore unexpected avenues to find new customers.

4. Be experimental
Find out what works through trial and error.

5. Be first
Lead the way and ensure you appear as a thought leader in your sector.

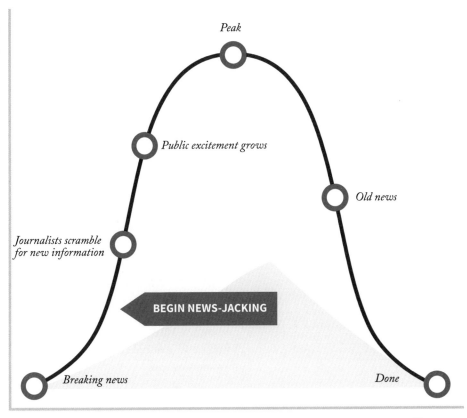

To **YouTube** or not to **YouTube?**

To YouTube

When you're looking to generate referral traffic and maximise your brand exposure online, YouTube is one of the best places to do this. It's currently the second largest search engine in the world and there's no sign of this changing any time soon.

If your audience responds particularly well to video, building your own YouTube channel should be a priority. The name of the game here is to build subscribers that regularly check out your content each time you publish something new.

If there's already a number of successful YouTube channels talking about your subject matter, don't be discouraged. It shows there's a demand for what you're doing and also highlights some great places to start talking to people and networking to build your own channel. YouTubers quite often collaborate or give shout outs to each other, which is a very good way to help each other build a following.

To not YouTube

YouTube is a phenomenal video hosting and search platform with some undeniable benefits including visibility and traffic generation as a result. However, there are a couple of reasons to use a different video hosting technique which should be considered before you decide which way to go.

1. Appearance: YouTube offers a number of crude setting options but it doesn't always look great on a webpage. It can look slightly unprofessional when compared to hosting through your own site.

2. On-page SEO: If you host all of your videos on YouTube and simply embed the video within a web page, guess who benefits from the video views from an SEO point of view – YouTube does! By hosting your own video on a web page, you get the SEO benefit (We recommend having a transcription of your video content underneath if possible too).

3. Analytics: If your video is a crucial element in a sales funnel of any kind, it's important you know how hard it's working for you. By using a platform such as Wistia to host your video on your website, you can get access to a whole host of very interesting data to help you assess how your video is performing.

4. If your audience is largely on Facebook, getting video views on this channel should be your number one priority. By uploading your content directly to Facebook it will be favoured up to six times more than an embedded YouTube video. In addition, the auto-play feature is enabled and the experience for the user is simpler and more enjoyable. You can also embed your Facebook video in other places just like you can with YouTube videos – such as your blog, for example.

5. If your audience is largely on Twitter you may want to follow the same advice as above, but this time you can upload using Vine.

How to use video to
get a huge return

Research shows that for businesses online, one minute of video can be worth up to 1.8 million written words. It's one of the most powerful digital mediums available to marketers, forecast to account for 84% of internet traffic by 2018 – so it's not to be underestimated.

On average, 68% of customers share a video they've watched and they're 78% more likely to buy something if they watch a video that showcases it first – but how can you ensure that yours is one of them?

1. Combine data and creativity

100 hours of video are uploaded to YouTube every minute. That's 144,000 hours of competition for your content. Don't get lost in the crowd. Make sure you optimise your content by using the same technical SEO techniques we discussed earlier. Ensure you research the best titles and keywords to include in your description and tag the video appropriately, so it's more likely to be found.

2. Engage an emotional response

Hold your audience's attention using pathos – a direct appeal to their emotions – giving them a reason to share your content. This is where you use your persona research to really nail the type of content that your target audience will engage with. Your video should be designed with a persona and an end goal in mind – otherwise it's just noise. To be remarkable, you have to stack the odds in your favour and do your homework properly. The silver bullet is in undertaking the hard work at the planning phase.

3. Go mobile

92% of mobile video viewers have shared some of the content they view. Make sure your videos and the places they are hosted are viewable on any mobile device and easily sharable.

4. Time it right

Using analytics to discover when and where your audience is active online will impact engagement levels and could even see you on YouTube's leaderboard! Improve your chances of being discovered by promoting your video when the majority of your audience are actually online. Lots of tools will help you do this including Hootsuite, Social Bro and HubSpot.

5. Seed, seed, seed

Give your video content some momentum by making it visible to the individuals who influence your audience. By creating your video with a particular persona in mind, you should easily be able to identify key individuals that create the perfect target audience to introduce your content to. A good way to do this is to 'influence your influencer'.

6. Influence your influencer

Sometimes it's easier to get your influencer's attention by seeing who it is they engage with most. This might not necessarily be an individual with the most followers or greatest social reach. A great tool for finding this kind of information is Mentionmapp. com. It gives you a visual link between influencers and their community and highlights the strongest and most frequent connections in a very clear way.

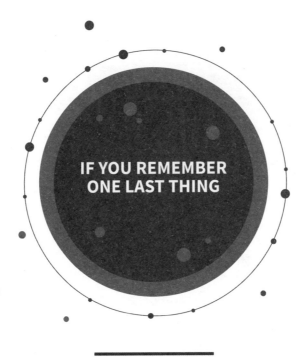

IF YOU REMEMBER ONE LAST THING

There are no shortcuts for creating great content, especially when you're looking to add value and drive your plan forward strategically.

The more you consider what your audience really wants — and the greater the lengths you go to in order find out exactly what that is — the better your results will be.

Doing something properly is worth 100,000 times the value of doing something quickly. Only with practice and an efficient process will you be able to achieve both.

Content calendar guideline download

Download our guide template for content creation at the link below to ensure you're planning your content effectively and reaching your overall business objectives.

ph-creative.com/Chapter7Resources

Key takeaways for chapter 7: part 1

By this point you should have your content planned and your strategy should be starting to come together. But it's important to consider your tactics before you leap into your strategy. Check off each of the points below as you complete them, to make sure you're on track.

☐ Review your current content – what's worked and what hasn't?

☐ Ego-jack your relevant influences with listicles, infographics and other content

☐ Schedule news-jacking into your content plan

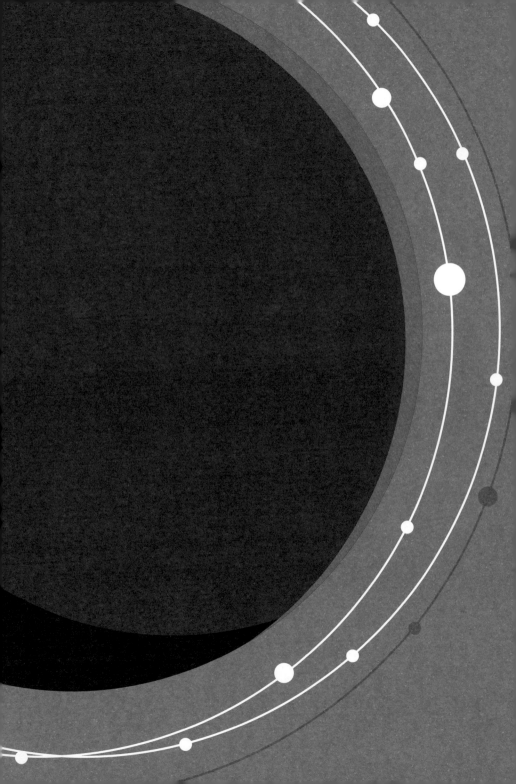

CHAPTER 7: part 2
THE MASTER PLAN

Implementing your marketing plan successfully is, without a doubt, one of the most important elements within your strategy. We understand that this chapter is a little long, so we've split it into two parts to make it easier to digest.

So let's start with paying to play and then we'll move on to breaking down the benefits of each social channel so you can start leveraging winning tactics for yourself.

Paying to play

Most major social media platforms are now, without a doubt, PLCs. Every key player is in this game for the profit and that's the stark truth we all need to accept.

Until recently, many brands succeeded in building vast social media audiences and marketing to them for free. But the social media giants have caught on, and reach has never been as restricted as it is now.

Starbucks is probably one of the best examples of this approach. They have built well over 10 million Facebook fans and every day, despite being a multi-billion dollar organisation, Facebook allowed them to market and engage with their audience in a very effective and efficient way.

If Starbucks gave out a 'free muffin' voucher on a Wednesday morning via Facebook, people around the world, in their millions, would go and redeem that offer. Of course, they would also be likely to buy a premium drink while they're in there – who eats a muffin without a coffee, right?

This generates fantastic customer satisfaction, engagement and a nice little spike of additional coffee sales to boot. Clever stuff.

Can you imagine something similar in the real world providing as much value? It's the equivalent of having access to every billboard in the world for 20 minutes one morning. In fact, it's much more powerful than that – who looks at billboards anymore? Now, however, Starbucks can post content to their Facebook page for free but the difference is, only around 6% of fans will see it. If they want to reach the rest, they have to pay. And so do we.

But it's not all bad news. There are many upsides to the changing digital landscape. In 2000, Google literally shook the marketing world with their advertising platform, Google AdWords. Providing advertisers with the ability to put offers in front of people actively searching for their products and services introduced a whole new method of targeting. This was controlled by matching your adverts to the keywords that your audience typed into the search box of Google.

If that wasn't good enough already, you only paid when someone actually clicked on a link. Instead of paying for people to passively view your advert, you only paid for engagement. Unbelievable!

This was a game changer of monumental proportions. Google AdWords was hailed the most measurable, reliable, accurate and targeted form of advertising to ever exist. Competition for keywords was also extremely low in the beginning, meaning that each keyword had a significantly lower bid price. Now, the same keywords are still being used by advertisers to drive traffic to websites, but those keywords are much more expensive. As an example, 'personal injury claims' was around 25p in 2002. Today it can be over £100 per click. Ouch.

Google AdWords is still going strong, but now it has competition. It was the AdWords model that shaped how online platforms offer their paid promoted services. Yet these social platforms have become a whole lot smarter too.

The exciting thing for us all is, without a doubt, the fact that history has a habit of repeating itself. Just like the cost of Google AdWords campaigns in 2000, social media paid promotion is extremely cheap compared to where it will be in just a few short years. Now is the time to invest. Now is the time to take advantage of the 'golden years' of social media promotion. Trust us, there will never be a better time to play online than right now.

If you're still a little upset about it not being free anymore, we have further good news to cheer you up. Instead of paying to just reach your existing fans and followers, all of the major social platforms (and very soon Instagram and Pinterest) have opened up their marketplace so you can target users of the entire platform. This is exciting. It's a monumental game changer that, frankly, blows Google AdWords out of the water.

To highlight the shift in advertising opportunities, we're going to use Facebook as our primary example. It should be noted that all social platforms are following suit with exactly the same features.

Rest assured, if you read the following passage about Facebook and you don't think your audience is on Facebook, our advice is this: first of all, check that your assumption is correct. You may well be surprised by what you find. We've seen significant ROI for B2C brands but also B2B business selling products and services such as insurance, business banking, legal services and even engineering services on the platform. Secondly, if you are right we can guarantee the opportunities exist on your platform of choice. Twitter and LinkedIn both have similarly incredible advertising and content promotion features that can deliver just as high conversion rates.

Paying to play: **Facebook**

Paying to play on Facebook comes in two forms, the traditional ad and the unpublished 'dark' post.

The unpublished 'dark' post allows you to create multiple adverts to promote through your page. But unlike a traditional ad, it won't show up on your main profile news feed, instead it shows up only in the feeds of those you've targeted.

Traditional ads can be targeted to where they will appear within a user's feed, but they will also appear on your profile page. This limits your options for split testing and distributing ads at scale as every variant will be published to your news feed – potentially alienating target groups who visit your profile page. If a post does fairly well organically on your page it might be worth then boosting the content to reach a wider audience.

The unpublished 'dark' post feature offers a subtle difference to the above. It's more significant than any other form of marketing the world has ever seen.

Does that sound a little dramatic? Possibly over stated? Perhaps, but consider this: you now have the flexibility to design multiple iterations of a post and split test this content to an audience that you define – with laser targeted precision.

Your options are not limited to just gender, age, location, or interests; you can even segment an audience based on previous purchasing behaviour.

In our agency, we're seeing traditional monthly AdWords budgets that have been performing well for years being poured into Facebook dark posts instead. In many cases, overnight the ROI goes up by more than five times.

For a long time, marketers have believed that Google AdWords is more effective than other paid advertising methods, specifically because of the intent behind user activity. By showing ads based on searched for keywords, it stands to reason that audiences will be more likely to click an advert, because of its relevance.

While this is still true, the options for using paid promotion across social channels are expanding, providing more targeting options which quantify your audience to perhaps an even more targeted level than Google AdWords.

Facebook Custom Audiences

Facebook's Custom Audience feature is another tool in their advertising armoury that helps you market with sniper-grade accuracy. This tool takes targeting your audience to the next level, allowing you ultimate control over who sees your ads.

The possibilities for this tool are endless and should definitely be explored. Whether you're looking to net customers who have subscribed to your newsletters or promotions or looking to gain repeat customers, the Custom Audiences tool is a simply brilliant tactic to employ.

Custom Audiences allow you to create your own audience for each of your Facebook adverts – made up of any marketing list that you have complied. These lists can be formed from your exported LinkedIn contacts, or you can even assign the hard work to Facebook and mine information from your website or mobile app. Basically, any list you create, which includes email addresses or phone numbers, can be used to create a Custom Audience.

Custom Audiences can also help you to market to your customers based on their exact point in the buying cycle. For example, an individual who is currently at the 'think' stage in the funnel could see a different (and ultimately more relevant ad) than an individual at the 'delight' stage. Therefore, if you're marketing a 20% discount offer, an individual who is at the 'see' stage may be targeted with an offer for new customers, whereas an individual at the 'delight' stage be targeted with an offer for returning/ loyal customers.

Meeting the needs of the people

It's fair to say that people's online browsing habits are experiencing a massive shift. It is no longer simply a case of people networking on social platforms and buying on specific websites anymore. We are online 24/7 and we buy where we see good value.

Strengthening its hold on ecommerce even further, Facebook has recently announced its new marketing platform, Atlas. The latest initiative from Facebook is a drive to encourage retailers selling in high street shops to share their sales data with Facebook in order to better inform them of what we're buying. This is to allow retailers to find additional value when targeting the same customer via Facebook and join up the 'real world' experience with the online one.

The obvious analogy to draw between Facebook's assault on Google's territory is that of Blackberry and Apple. When Blackberry's confidence in dominating the business phone market was at its height, Apple introduced the iPhone.

When Apple released the iPhone, Blackberry were confident that it had the business market sealed with a stronghold that would be difficult to disrupt. While Apple focused

on the sociable aspects of their device; music, games, video, messaging etc. Blackberry doubled down on the business applications and traded on their email provision and other productivity-focused features.

You could be forgiven for looking at this landscape and predicting people may use the new iPhone for pleasure but the Blackberry would always be the business weapon of choice. How wrong we were.

Apple focused on the person first, specific uses second. The CEO, manager, executive and the receptionist are all people with families and family lives. Apple started with 'why' and told a story of how intuitive the iPhone was to use and painted a picture of how cool it was to have an one. This quickly saw it become a must-have lifestyle accessory.

Meanwhile, Blackberry continues to cling to the features and the 'what' but suffer the consequences of ignoring the wants, needs and desires of their audience.

Facebook are quietly doing exactly the same as Apple. They've dominated their space by giving their audience what they want for years and now they're closing in on the business side of their platform with a tidal wave of success.

Leveraging best practice techniques within the social channels

Trend-jacking for maximum effect on Twitter

Twitter is one of the best platforms for engaging with your customers when it comes to real-time and current events. A platform which is built around listening to others and sharing opinions in bite size format, it's fantastic for boosting engagement.

Through searching and hashtagging appropriately, you can find and get involved in up-to-date conversations and topical issues.

Trend-jacking (using a hashtag to promote your brand) can be a great way to gain exposure and get your message seen by thousands. But beware, if not utilised properly, this can backfire and damage your reputation, so be careful!

Make sure you've thoroughly researched the meaning of the hashtag you intend to trend-jack, ensure it is relevant to your brand, find out what people are saying about the hashtag and make sure you can fit into their conversations.

Finally, establish whether using it will positively impact your brand. If you can't justify using it, or it's not relevant, steer clear. Audiences will see through inauthentic attempts at trend exploitation – don't appear

desperate and only use a hashtag if you have 100% clarity it will be a good move.

A good example of a brand effectively engaging in trend-jacking is Snickers' campaign during the FIFA World Cup in 2014. During the match between Uruguay and Italy, it appeared that Luis Suarez, the Uruguay striker, had bitten another player during a tackle.

In a swift and clever move, which completely resonated with the brand, values and humour, Snickers posted a photo tweet using the hashtag #luissuarez. So perfect was the timing, sentiment and message, it got retweeted nearly 50,000 times.

Get the most out of **Facebook**

As we've discussed, Facebook is a great platform for promoting content due to its ultra-targeted nature, particularly with the unpublished 'dark' post. However, it's not enough to simply post content and hope that it will do well.

As with all of your content, you need to make sure it fits with your brand values, your objectives and most importantly, your audience. 63% of Facebook users engage on a daily basis, so you need to ensure your posts are a part of this statistic.

Whether you're paying to play, or posting organically, you need to ensure that you've thought through every element of your Facebook posts, from fantastic imagery, to engaging copy and a clear call to action. Do this and you'll achieve maximum clicks, engagement and shares on the platform.

One brand that utilises Facebook very well is Oreo. Using a mixture of timely trend-jacking and down-to-earth posts to boost engagement, Oreo knows exactly who its customers are and plays to this.

The example to the right showcases Oreo's ability to present exactly what its audience

responds to. Through a simple image and a tongue in cheek description Oreo generated over 20,000 likes and 1,200 shares. How did they do it?

> Like   Comment
>
> Oreo
> Oh, you like penguins? That's cute.
>
> Album: Timeline Photos
> Shared with: Public

By recognising a trend and putting their own spin on it. At the time of posting, John Lewis's 'Monty the Penguin' advert was generating traction on social media. Oreo responded in a way that uniquely showcased its brand and subtly alluded to the advert, without needing to jump onto hashtags or even include a direct reference. It's simply brilliant.

Maximise referrals with **Pinterest**

With its easy to consume, visual interface, Pinterest is a fantastic place for you to showcase your brand's services and benefits.

Pinterest allows users to compile and follow visual boards of their favourite things – from wedding inspiration, to photography, to the places they'd like to visit. Unlike any other social network, Pinterest allows users to define their life, ambitions, desires and choices using images alone – all while providing a direct link back to the original publisher of the content.

Many brands are already capitalising on the popularity of this social network, creating visually stunning content which gets pinned thousands of times over – providing them with thousands of referrals directly back to their product(s).

Many marketers fail to use Pinterest, believing it is a platform only for women – mistakenly thinking that if they aren't selling food, clothes or wedding supplies, they'll fall flat. This is certainly not the case.

The ability to create boards means that users can follow your individual boards – not just you as a brand – allowing you to segment products and services into tailored groups, which, when tagged effectively, can hit multiple target personas. It's important to remember though, as Pinterest is a visual platform – no matter how many keywords you use, or tags you include, if your image is shoddy, it's not going to do well.

Ben & Jerry's is the perfect example of a brand that uses Pinterest effectively. While it recognises the highly visual, female-dominated use of the platform, the brand also includes a host of other interesting boards to appeal to a wider demographic.

From 'Fan Photos' to its 'On a Mission' board, which showcases its involvement in gay rights and fair trade issues, Ben & Jerry's has all of its bases covered. Combine this with striking, high resolution images and you have a recipe for success every time.

Tell your story on
YouTube

YouTube can be an extremely valuable channel to include in your inbound marketing strategy – if used correctly. If you need a recap on what makes a good YouTube video, skip back a few pages to refresh your memory.

There are some fantastic examples of brands using YouTube to promote their content and the good news is their success is easy to replicate. Unlike a TV ad, creating content for YouTube doesn't necessarily have to be high budget or have high production values in order to do well on the platform.

A brilliant example of a brand using YouTube well is Blendtec. Their most popular product is a blender, boldly labelled 'the worlds' most advanced blender'. So what did Blendtec do to showcase their product on YouTube? They blended stuff. Everything from iPhones to diamonds. They created a story from a unique selling point.

Why was it so successful? Because it provided not only something interesting to watch, but it gave audiences a reason to keep coming back, time after time, to see what they would blend next. Keeping its videos timely – by blending items such as the latest iPad model (gaining over 17 million views) – a simple concept has the ability to be used for years to come (and all at a relatively low cost).

Check it out now – we guarantee you won't be able to watch just one video. You can find this video, plus all your other resources for this chapter by visiting the link below. **ph-creative.com/Chapter7Resources**

Reach millennials with **Snapchat**

This fledgling platform has been gaining traction with the millennial demographic for quite some time. Whilst many marketers feel that this platform isn't relevant to their audience, statistics beg to differ.

With 400 million snaps sent daily and under-25s accounting for 71% of their user base, this platform can be a fantastic tool for engaging with a younger audience.

If you're going to begin using Snapchat, remember who your audience is and tailor your content to fit. Snapchat works by providing bite size visual chunks of information – so remember to keep it relevant.

Wordy sales pitches or product demos won't work on this platform; be creative and do your research into what performs well and what doesn't. Be humorous and light-hearted – a younger demographic love to be entertained so remember this.

Audi has recently used Snapchat to great effect as part of their advertising efforts. During the Superbowl, its engaged with its audience through creating funny, photo-captioned snaps that resonated perfectly with a younger audience.

By creating in-the-moment content, paired with humour and stock photos, Audi not only gained traction through Snapchat, but the momentum spilled over onto other platforms too – getting multiple audiences talking about their interactions.

Showcase your products through **Instagram**

Instagram is fast becoming one of the most sought after social media platforms for brands to showcase themselves. Instagram has recently rolled out advertising options for businesses, meaning that it just got a whole lot more attractive for marketers.

The bottom line in using this platform effectively is in the quality of the images you post. Instagram, like Pinterest, is highly visual – users respect and respond to artful and well considered imagery that doesn't feel commercialised. To be successful on this platform, you need to ensure that you're authentic and respect what it is that your followers want to see.

A brand that harnesses the power of Instagram particularly well is Starbucks. Starbucks manages all of its social channels very effectively, but Instagram stands out as one of its strongest. Starbucks often 'regrams' photos posted by fans, boosting engagement levels and showing true, human interactions, making the brand feel authentic and honest.

Alongside this, it regularly posts beautifully composed and edited images, which is exactly what users are looking for. By using careful hashtags that only apply to the Starbucks brand (for example #PSL – pumpkin spice latte), it ensures that their posts are never spammy or appear to be trend-jacking unnecessarily.

Explore the features on **G+**

G+ is an often overlooked platform in the social media armoury, but can be of huge benefit to your inbound strategy. Whilst many see the platform as a place to duplicate Facebook or Twitter messages, it has many individual attributes which can, and should, be utilised.

With additional features such as Google Hangouts and the ability to share locations, G+ can really boost a brand's social media presence and Search Engine Results Page (SERP) ranking when used correctly. G+ can also be brilliant for extending your business network through using its Circles feature. Through this, you can categorise your connections and control who sees your updates. For example, if you're promoting a service only available to other businesses, you can post an update to your 'business' circle.

Through utilising the G+ Hangouts feature, car manufacturer Toyota created a unique 'collaborator area'; a digital space where up to five people can collaborate on creating and designing a new Toyota. The finished car can even be taken for a virtual test-drive on Google Maps. This concept is unique to G+ and so brings new potential customers to their platform, while also providing a unique and novel way to keep them there.

Get audience-centric using **Tumblr**

The microblogging platform Tumblr is relatively new territory for brands, but when utilised well, it can be extremely beneficial.

As it currently stands, only 31 of the top 100 global brands have a Tumblr account – which is good news if you're looking to beat the competition.

When implementing a strategy for the platform, place a heavy focus on the right kinds of imagery – 78% of posts on Tumblr are photos or images. Hone in on your target audience to find your own niche. Tumblr is made up of small communities – understanding the humour and tone they

adopt will mean your content is successful time and time again. Of all the social platforms, Tumblr sees the highest amount of GIF shares, so consider this where possible.

Lana Del Rey's Tumblr page is a fantastic example of the platform being used to engage and publicise. To promote her latest single, she posted short GIFs of her upcoming music video to the site, with fantastic results. Her audience responded to this kind of content as it correlated with what they like to share and discuss across the platform.

LANA DEL REY

Boost your engagement levels by saying **Ello**

Ello may be arriving late to the social media cocktail party but with sign-ups reaching 38,000 per hour at its busiest, this platform is generating enough buzz for brands to start taking it seriously.

As an ad-free social network, you could be forgiven for assuming that there is no place for your brand on the platform. But that's not the case. Although not as sophisticated as Facebook, there are still plenty of opportunities for brands looking to connect and engage.

Being successful on Ello does, however, require you to change the way you think about your social media strategy. Not being able to pay to play means that only those who actively choose to follow you will see your updates – creating a much smaller audience, who are genuinely interested in your brand.

This can be a great platform for identifying and engaging with your brand advocates – just make sure you're posting authentic and genuine content. Much like Tumblr, Ello thrives on small niche communities. You need to find yours and engage with them regularly. Every aspect of Ello has been considered and designed in order to be clean and crisp – cutting out the clutter of many of our current social networks. Remember this when posting content to the network: use vivid, clear and high resolution images alongside minimal text.

Marketing, media and advertising publication Adweek is an early adopter of Ello as a social platform. Combining a mix of its usual posts (like latest articles) with GIFs and posts just for fun, Adweek actively captures the attention of those that follow the brand. Ello shows a view count underneath every post – Adweek's view count regularly matches and exceeds their total amount of followers.

Blog your way to more customers with **Medium**

Medium – founded by Biz Stone and Twitter's former CEO, Evan Williams, in August 2012 – is an interesting place for a brand to build a community.

Rather than the popularity of the author, Medium rewards content for quality and relevance, over any other factors. Categorising content into collections, Medium makes it easy for users to search and find what they are looking for.

Medium, like other smaller social networks, is used by a variety of niche communities, so you need to find one which will respond well to your brand and content. Rather than using Medium for marketing alone, you could try using it to test out your content before posting it to your blog, or just to prove your expertise in a subject area.

It's a good idea to post as an individual on behalf of a brand rather than posting as a brand as an entity. This hikes up the 'relatability factor' of your written content – people often like to associate a face and a name to the things they read. This has the added benefit of distancing your blogs from simple marketing material, positioning them as genuine and engaging pieces of writing.

Gary Vaynerchuk has enthusiastically adopted Medium to further cement his brand presence. Regularly posting genuinely useful content aimed at solving audience pain points, his presence on Medium is strong without feeling like he's constantly trying to sell something. If you're looking to start posting your own content on Medium, his profile wouldn't be a bad place to start when looking for inspiration.
medium.com/@garyvee

Gary Vaynerchuk
Family 1st but after that, Businessman, Tweeting at @garyvee and working at @vaynermedia. Tasted wine for years online!

FOLLOWING 3.2K   FOLLOWERS 44K   ELSEWHERE

Follow

MOST RECOMMENDED

The Leverage of Being a Good Person
GARY VAYNERCHUK 2 min read

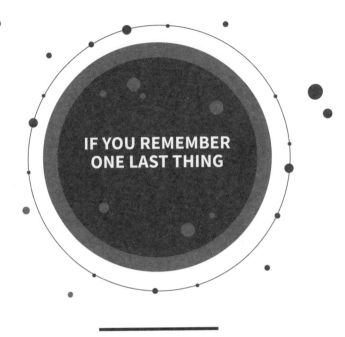

IF YOU REMEMBER
ONE LAST THING

This is the part where we sneak in a word about budget.

If, after reading this chapter, you're not convinced you should budget for paid social promotion to win new customers, then you may look back on ignoring our advice with regret.

It's cheaper now than it will be in the very near future, so make sure you reap the rewards.

Recommended reading & resources

ONLINE

Sniply

Sniply allows you to shorten URLs and drive traffic to your own site with every link you share. Add a call-to-action banner to every URL link and get rewarded for sharing great content.
snip.ly

HubSpot

Having coined the term 'Inbound Marketing', HubSpot has created one of the best tools in the business to enhance your inbound marketing strategy. Helping you to identify and maximise your buyer personas, attract visitors, convert leads and close customers, it pretty much does it all. Invaluable for digital marketers.
hubspot.com

Topsy

Topsy, a certified Twitter partner, is a social search and analytics company. It maintains a catalogue of tweets dating back to Twitter's launch in 2006. Topsy allows you to analyse keywords and authors by a series of conditions.
topsy.com

Feedly

Feedly is a tool which makes organising, reading and sharing content easier. You are able to search for specific keywords and start creating a library of information to share across your social media channels.
feedly.com

SocialBro

With SocialBro at your fingertips you can analyse and manage your Twitter audience. There are a whole host of features available that will make your overall job easier. From identifying influencers to finding the best time to tweet, SocialBro can help.
socialbro.com

Infogr.am

With over 2,000,000 infographics created since its launch in 2012, Infogr.am brings out the best in the data you have. You can create and share infographics, online charts and data visualisations.
infogr.am

Hootsuite

This social media management system supports all your social media platforms from Twitter and Facebook to Google+ and Foursquare, helping you keep track and manage your social media channels. Monitoring interactions, Hootsuite enables you to respond instantly.

hootsuite.com

Bitly

Bitly is a tool allowing you to easily save and share links across your social channels. The URL shortening service, which was established in 2008, shortens more than one billion links per month.

bitly.com

Hemingwayapp

A useful tool for exploring how easy to read your content is, Hemingwayapp breaks down where you're going wrong with your content. Insert just a few sentences or an entire essay and let the software analyse any weak points within your writing. Perfect for content marketers searching for crisp, clear copy.

hemingwayapp.com

Trello

Keep track of all of your daily, weekly and monthly tasks, create collaborative areas and visually tick things off of your to do list. Keeping you on track, no matter what your team size, Trello is a must for any business looking to stay organised.

trello.com

Future of social download

Download our Future of social media ebook by visiting the link below. Start understanding how you can use social media to positively connect and engage with your audience and start adding value to your social interactions.

ph-creative.com/Chapter7Resources

Key takeaways for chapter 7: part 2

Ensure that you're crafting relevant content for your audience based on the social channels you have selected. Consider different messaging for each platform and innovative ways of making each of your selected channels relevant to your audience through utilising their unique features.

☐ Tweak the content that didn't work to target your personas

☐ Mark which social tactics and platforms are relevant for your personas

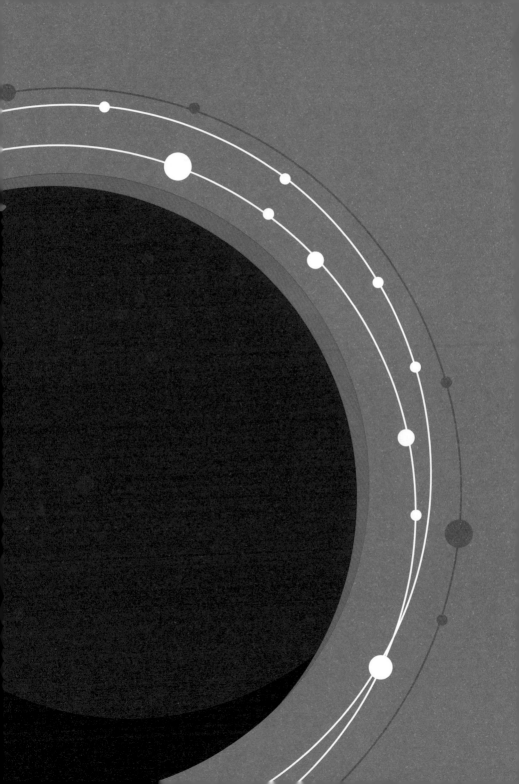

TOOLS FOR THE JOB

What to measure and how to measure it to determine what matters and how to deliver the success you're looking for.

"Success is a lousy teacher. It seduces smart people into thinking they can't lose."
Bill Gates

"Marketing is too important to be left to the marketing department."
David Packard

"An ounce of performance is worth pounds of promise."
Mae West

"In this day and age, there's no excuse for marketing in the dark when it comes to measuring your effectiveness."

Let's face it, getting goosebumps from your inbound marketing is utopian and not always possible the first time you publish new content. You might very well get it slightly wrong a few times before you nail it and get the reaction you're looking for – that's very common.

It is more than achievable though, which is why we maintain it should be your ultimate goal when adding value for the different personas of your audience.

Running a digital agency for over ten years, we've noticed that clients tend to be infinitely more interested in the detail of weekly and monthly reports when something is going wrong, rather than when a campaign is performing off the chart – it's human nature.

More often than not, when a strategy is performing to plan, clients tend to enjoy talking about future activities; chatting to us about strategic goals and new ways to grow their online estate. Even with the hard facts in a report, more often than not it's your intuition that first assesses the situation. You must listen to your gut. If your content isn't giving you goosebumps it's probably not going to set your audience's world on fire either.

We've talked at length about how hard it is to craft content that will resonate with your audience as well as lead them closer towards a goal. This stuff isn't easy to master and there are no shortcuts. If you've done your homework and you understand and care about your audience sufficiently to begin with, you should already know, to a certain degree, how successful a piece of content will be before you push it out to the big wide world. But sometimes, you're not right. Sometimes the complete opposite happens. Content that you were certain would do well can completely fail and vice versa.

Even if you're right 75% of the time, that's not good enough. Just like it's not good enough to drive a car and get to your destination just 75% of the time.

The following analogy of a car is an interesting one and accurately helps to describe the way most businesses drive their marketing, each and every day.

If you had to drive 100 miles to a distant relative's house for the holidays and you rented a car with no speedo, no petrol gauge, no SatNav and no mirrors, how confident would you be in getting to your destination safely?

That's how many businesses run their marketing department – the engine works, the tyres are good and the car seems to really move forward well – there's even someone behind the wheel that seems to be a really good driver. But are we burning too much fuel? Are we going in the right direction? Are we wasting time and resource that could be deployed differently?

The answer is yes. In this day and age, there are no excuses for marketing without a fully functioning dashboard. We've suggested lots of tools throughout this book that measure varying degrees of success for a variety of specific tactics and techniques. These tools are all of great value and we stand by them.

However, when it comes to the overview of your marketing activity, we highly recommend considering an investment in one marketing automation tool to give you clarity, consistency and effective intelligence across the board.

By assessing the contribution that your individual marketing activities make to your campaigns you can see what's working and what needs improving. You can also measure the ROI of each activity as well as gather an overall ROI of all of your marketing activity in total. Technology should be an enabler for your business. If technology is a cause of frustration in your business, it's the wrong tool for the job. For the good of your sanity, results and profit, get yourself the right tools.

In the interest of transparency, our agency is a HubSpot partner and so we strongly advocate using its particular marketing automation solution. However, there are other options and you have to find the right solution for your business.

It is worth pointing out however that the reason we're passionate about HubSpot is because of the significant benefits, results and intelligence we have gained through using it. We shopped around and made our choice very carefully after reviewing the options. Whichever solution you choose, just make sure you have the right tools to holistically manage your inbound marketing, effectively and efficiently.

What should you look for in a marketing automation solution to measure your digital marketing activity?

Areas of measurement you should look for in one tool

- Blogging & calls to action

- SEO

- CMS / landing pages

- Lead management

- Email marketing

- Analysis

- CRM integration

- Smart / dynamic downloads

Specific features you should look for to market smarter

- Keyword suggestion / grader

- Scheduling across multiple channels

- Page replication for quick execution

- Campaign tagging to measure social attribution

- Synchronised campaign analysis linked to other inbound activity

- Personalisation of pages, emails and general experience to maximise conversion

"If there's any doubt about the ROI of your marketing in any given month, you're doing it wrong."

A high proportion of marketing professionals fail to measure their marketing activities accurately. This can be easily forgiven and put right. It's when you're told that you can't measure your activity that you have a problem.

These days, inbound marketing offers unprecedented clarity and accuracy in terms of measuring the success of individual campaigns and indicating overall marketing ROI. Despite this, the number one question we face as an agency continues to be, 'what's the best way to measure social media ROI?'

In order to present a simple and coherent answer it's important to cast your mind back to the first couple of chapters. Without understanding what success looks like for your business, it's very difficult to tell you what success looks like when analysing your inbound marketing and social media activities.

What's the point in gaining 1,000 new Facebook likes every day if they don't add value to your business? It sounds good, but compared to what and for what purpose? On the flip side, if you do have this information all mapped out it's very easy, but all too often we see tactics being deployed without the strategy underpinning them.

Think back to the master timeline spreadsheet that maps everything from your business objectives to your business strategy, down to tactics and implementation. From here, it's a simple case of working backwards to reverse engineer what level of activity, engagement and conversion you need to hit the goals.

What is the value of a tweet on Twitter? In general, who knows? But, if you know that one of your target personas, at the THINK stage of your funnel, spends most time on Twitter and responds best at 7pm, when using the hashtag #marketingtips, then you can start to see the value of your efforts…

And if you know that for every tweet that includes a link, you typically get 200 click-throughs to your content, which in turn generates 10 downloads of an e-book, you now know that the tweet is worth 10 new contacts in your database.

If you also know that for every 250 new contacts in your database, you typically get five new sales opportunities from your email marketing of which you convert one sale worth £100, you now know that your one tweet is potentially worth £4.

10 (contacts) / (250 contacts needed to make a sale) x £100= £4

So what's the value of 1,000 Facebook fans? If you know you can sell £100 worth of products or services per 1,000 fans from your Facebook engagement, then you know each fan is worth 10p.

The power of Social
Attribution Modelling

I'm sure by now you get the general idea of how you can start to measure social media and inbound marketing activity to begin to formulate a meaningful ROI. However, it's not always as linear and simple as the examples on the previous page.

Sometimes people will click on a link in a tweet, land on your website and then leave. Those same customers could Google you a week later and click on an organic link (SEO) to find you again. It's equally possible that the next day they click an AdWords link (PPC) and then check you out on YouTube or Facebook before coming back and making a purchase.

It's exhausting just imagining that journey, but we all do it. On average a new visitor to a website needs to visit a website six times before making an initial purchase or enquiry.

Quite often, when measuring the effectiveness of marketing activities people will look at the sources of traffic to their website. It's quite simple to see in order of referral where your traffic is coming from.

It's quite a logical assumption that if Google AdWords (PPC) is converting the most traffic into leads and sales that AdWords is your most valuable traffic source. However, we're only accounting for the last click of what might be

a sporadic or varied journey to get to the final sales conversion, just like this example.

To get the full picture, we have to look at the complete end-to-end journey a prospect has taken to establish the true ROI of each channel and the effort you're spending in each.

If it turned out that in most cases, new sales or leads were landing because their first interaction with your brand was from a link to a blog post on Twitter, you're now seeing the full picture and starting to reassess the value of your Google AdWords campaign.

Every touch point with your brand that brings a prospect closer to making a purchase or submitting an enquiry on your website or social account has a value attributed to it based on the contribution it's made during that journey. **This is called social attribution.**

Being able to measure the complete social attribution of your leads or sales is paramount. It will shape your thinking and allow you to strategically plan your content in order to optimise your chances of landing new business.

Imagine trying to work out the value of each attribution by stitching various analytics together… Suddenly we're driving without a dashboard again. Having a software tool to stitch all of these moving parts together is crucial to any serious digital marketer.

Crucial? Why so serious? Your competition is getting smarter as well as working harder and these are the marginal gains you need to capitalise on right now. You've not got the time or the budget to compromise in this area.

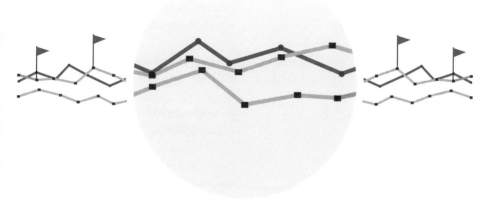

Becoming **mobile friendly**

There's a distinct 'anytime, anywhere' attitude to mobile device engagement. Google knows this and it wants to sell its services to consumers who are now as much (if not more) mobile users of its tools and products.

This directly impacts on how they are building out their plans around mobile device SEO and usability. Just check out 'Google Webmaster' and their views on usability in mobile browsers.

Remember, as the URL for a site can include the letter 'm' to indicate a mobile browser version, there are new pages to index and the competition for that visibility is also new (compared to that of the older desktop web page).

How mobile users interact with content is different, how they want it presented is different – and they are much more 'take action now' based. Getting your mobile SEO and content strategy right in this world is still up for grabs. As talent consumers, Gen-Y and Millenials expect this and will respond with enthusiasm to those who get it right.

Google AMP

What is Google AMP?
Last October, Google announced the launch of Accelerated Mobile Pages (AMP). AMPs are a super user-friendly framework that let anyone create a fast-loading mobile responsive web page. The key here is fast loading for the mobile generation.

The technical SEO benefits of AMP
Currently, having AMPs on your mobile site isn't an independent ranking factor. However page load speed and mobile responsiveness are. The main selling point of AMPs is the fact that they instantly improve both of these ranking factors. So if you're developing your mobile site using AMPs then you're likely to be blessed with higher ranking. This is simply because you've automatically improved your page load speed and mobile friendliness by using this clever tool!

Another **hidden benefit** of AMP content is the way in which it's displayed on search engine results pages. They are rendered as large carousels, carrying images on the front page of Google SERPs. This is automatically more visually appealing and more likely to draw a user's attention. Perfect if you're searching for talent in the recruitment space.

The candidate experience benefits of AMP

Refer back to the above! The faster a user can find the most relevant content - the better response your site will receive, especially from candidates.

People searching for jobs simply don't have time to spare. If they can't access the information they want quickly (basically, in the blink of an eye) then you've lost them forever. If you're in the business of hunting for top talent, you never know if the person navigating away from you could potentially be your dream hire - so don't lose them.

By serving content that is super relevant and loads speedily, you'll improve your users experience **and** make their job search a hell of a lot easier. Candidates will love you for it and this will make them more likely to carry on through the application process with you.

How to create a Google AMP page

Intrigued? We certainly were when we heard about the benefits that this new initiative can offer. If you want to get started but you're not sure how, Google has a great, step by step tutorial. In it you'll learn how to create a basic page, how to stage it, make sure it complies with AMP rules and set it live for publication on Google. Perfection.

Voice search SEO

Voice search is one of the quickly evolving areas of recruitment. Exploring this may seem a little daunting for some, but we strongly believe there

are many benefits of voice search that should be embraced.

Google rolled out Hummingbird on 30th August 2013, completely overhauling how its algorithm worked. Its purpose was to understand user intent and make sense of questions, as opposed to keywords. It was to gravitate more towards conversational search, which was needed to make Google's voice search more effective.

What is voice search?

Google Voice Search is a product that allows users to use Google Search by speaking on a mobile phone or computer. A user starts a search by saying "OK Google", followed by asking it a question. Thanks to Hummingbird, Google is able to understand the intent of a question and bring up the correct results.

For example, if you were to ask "How long do lions live for?", Google would understand that you want to know the average life span of a lion and answer accordingly. Intelligent stuff.

How do you optimise your website for Voice Search?

All of our websites are built with voice search in mind and there are three main criteria we look at:

Questions not keywords: People don't speak how they type. With voice search, people ask a question instead of typing in a phrase or keyword. We optimise your website to cater towards conversational questions as opposed to specific keywords.

For example:

"Liverpool pizza" would become: "Where can I find a good pizza in Liverpool?"

A comprehensive FAQ section in a conversational, Q&A format is vital for voice search, along with the research that goes into finding these questions.

Optimise for mobile: Google's voice search is mainly aimed at smartphone users. We ensure your website is 100% optimised for mobile and considered mobile friendly by Google.

Multilingual: A key point with voice search is that web users are going to prefer to search in their native language. We research your core demographics deeply, and whether there are international language considerations, and apply this to your site.

Tools to treasure

Here is your must-have list of useful tools, each designed to ease you through the ever-changing world of SEO:

SocialCrawlytics
An essential free tool in online research, SocialCrawlytics analyses URLs to establish how popular they have proved across the social space. This tool can also find influencers and work out how your competitors are doing.
socialcrawlytics.com

Answer the Public
The simple little tool allows you to type in keywords and phrases to discover the most popular questions people type into Google around those words. It's a great tool for sparking ideas on what to write about, because you're answering the questions your audience is already asking.
answerthepublic.com

Followerwonk
A nifty social media tool which allows users to search for keywords in Twitter users' biographies. Followerwonk is a fast and effective way to find your buyer personas influencers, or even just people who have the same interests as you.
followerwonk.com

MentionMapp
Using data from the Twitter API, MentionMapp loads each user's Twitter updates to find all interactions and hashtag mentions, displaying them in a web-like format. MentionMapp makes researching your audience and influencers simple, allowing you to embark on a journey of discovery through a web of conversations and interactions.
followerwonk.com

BuzzSumo

A great tool for finding influencers, BuzzSumo allows users to search for and filter influencers by their type. Influencer lists can be exported into an Excel file, which enables results to be filtered even further. The tool can also be used to find the most popular content around certain topic by searching a specific keyword and phrases.

buzzsumo.com

Nuzzel

Nuzzel is a useful tool for collating the stories and articles that have been shared by your friends on Facebook and Twitter. A social news aggregator, Nuzzel makes it simple to see what's important, without overwhelming you with too much data.

nuzzel.com

Moz

We're not afraid to say that Moz is pretty amazing. It can do almost anything, including managing campaigns, tracking keyword changes, research backlink strength and track competitors. It's a must for anyone who wants to do SEO the right way.

moz.com

SEMrush

SEM Rush is perfect for reports and audits. If you're just starting out and want to get a handle on how your site is currently performing – and most importantly what you should change – SEM is the site for you. Providing handy data charts and venn diagrams, it's one of the best ways to get off to a winning start.

semrush.com

Google Keyword Planner

This is the one and only keyword researching tool that we — and the vast majority of other SEOs — use. It's also a Google product (yay). Of course, there are other keyword tools available, but they mostly derive their technology directly from this one. This should be your first stop for researching trends, monitoring keyword search volume and establishing how difficult it will be to compete for certain keywords.

adwords.google.com/ko/KeywordPlanner/Home

What is your conversion rate?

The conversion rate is the percentage of users who take a desired action. The archetypical example of conversion rate is the percentage of website visitors who buy something on the site.

A hugely important aspect in measuring the results of your inbound marketing is determining and refining your conversion rate from start to finish for each campaign.

It can sometimes be quicker, easier and cheaper to improve your ROI by increasing your website conversion rate from 4% to 5% of 10,000 visitors than it might be to generate an extra 2,500 visitors to get the same number of sales at the original 4% conversion rate.

Ideally, we'd like to increase both traffic and conversion rate. However, it's not worth fighting for more traffic when a website simply doesn't convert as well as it could if some minor changes were made.

If you owned a corner shop and noticed that the average customer spends £15 when they buy something at the checkout, but 19 out of every 20 people walk in and walk straight back out again, would you:

A) Stand on the street corner hustling more people into your shop?

B) Experiment with more impulse purchases at the checkout to improve the average basket value?

C) Or find out why 95% of your prospective customers change their mind and walk out so quickly after entering your shop?

Which one would you choose? I hope you chose C. It's a no-brainer, right?

To fix this hypothetical issue you might try some or all of the following tactics:

- Ask your customers what they like and dislike about the shopping experience

- Examine your signage to make it more obvious what you sell

- Change the appearance of the shop to be more relevant and appealing to your audience

- Examine the isles of the shop to make sure they're tidy, organised and clearly labelled so items are easy to find

- Make sure your items are grouped properly so shopping is fairly intuitive and easy to navigate around the shop, based on what you're looking for.

- Experiment with offers and messaging at the entrance to entice more people to start shopping

- Assess your shop assistants to ensure they're being helpful and pleasant with your customers

- Examine your advertising and marketing to make sure what you're using to drive people into your shop is consistent with what they find when you walk through the doors.

Does that sound about right? With your website and inbound marketing you can do exactly the same thing.

There are various tools that will help give you valuable insights into exactly what's going on within your website and how your website is performing in terms of customer experience. Google Analytics is probably the easiest and most common tool to use to set up basic goals to begin measuring how people are manoeuvring around your website and how many of these visitors are seeing the content you want them to see.

Just like a shop keeper might plan how they want visitors to navigate a physical shop to optimise the buying experience, you can do the same by choosing critical pages within your website to track and measure by setting 'goals' in Google Analytics.

Once you have goals set up you can begin to measure the efficiency of your website. If 90% of people are visiting your homepage and then clicking on a link to a page that doesn't add any value to your business, you can then start to change the on-site experience to divert traffic elsewhere.

It isn't hard to see how activity such as this has added £1,000s to many clients' bottom line very quickly, without waiting for more significant volumes of new traffic to build on their websites.

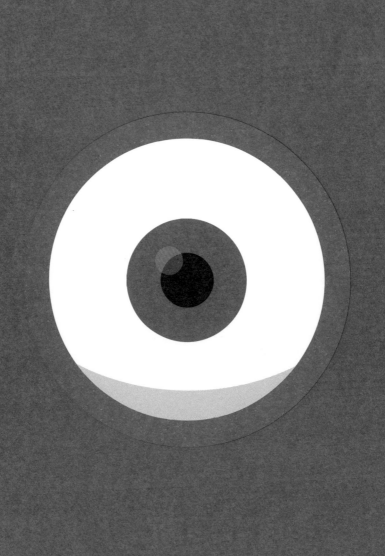

Heat mapping and eye tracking

Another way you can establish the behaviour of the individuals that land on your page is through heat mapping and eye tracking. Heat mapping and eye tracking allow you to clearly see which areas of your website are being clicked on or looked at most. This means you can optimise the layout of your website for higher conversion rate.

Although this can be an expensive process to undertake yourself, you can learn from other published eye tracking results to give you a general idea of best practice for website content placement.

Measuring tools you should consider using to improve your marketing efforts

Throughout this book, we've made reference to a host of relevant resources following every chapter and this chapter will be no different. However, to clarify and provide a better understanding of how to measure your efforts, each major social platform's analytics software is broken down into key considerations, pros and cons on the next few pages.

Google Analytics

In the absence of marketing automation software, Google Analytics provides some basic assisted conversions and attribution modelling data. You can use this data to track the contribution of all of your digital activity towards the specific goals you define. Getting to know the basics of Google Analytics is a very worthwhile exercise. Experiment with setting various goals within your website, depending on how your traffic flows from one page to another.

Each social media platform also has its own version of analytics and so, independently of each other, you can track and monitor the performance of each channel.

The difference between monitoring each channel separately and monitoring end-to-end campaigns is simply the ability to measure tactics when they're separate. You can measure the effectiveness of your entire strategy when they're all linked together with a more sophisticated software tool.

Pros
- Can import data from other sources
- Can easily be linked with any of your other Google products
- Continuously developed to improve
- Free online training available
- Create custom reports
- Track your own defined goals
- Can be linked with Google Adwords

Cons
- Maximum of 20 goals
- Upgrading to Premium is expensive
- Constant development requires constant training

Twitter Analytics

Twitter Analytics is available to all users, not just advertisers and verified account holders. This means you can track and understand the performance of every tweet you post. Displaying all of your metrics in a dashboard format, you can view your activity, follower demographics and monitor your promoted content (if you're using paid promotion).

Pros

- Simple interface makes it easy to break down your performance
- See how your followers are engaging with you in real time
- Downloadable tweet metrics
- See your followers' top interests
- View hashtag comparisons
- Monitor your engagements over a 28 day period

Cons

- Oversimplified for many marketers' needs
- Not sophisticated enough for deep historical metric analysis
- Some discrepancies between mentions, replies and retweets

Twitter Ad Manager

If you're looking to pay to promote your content on Twitter, their Ad Manager platform is a useful tool to help you understand the ways in which your paid content is performing.

Pros

- Keep a track of your budget and spend
- Understand your audience breakdown
- See the impressions/clicks/views/retweets of your promoted tweets

Cons

- Not as robust as Google Analytics
- Difficult to set up campaigns to run on certain days or during certain hours of individual days
- Bids need to be adjusted manually

Facebook Insights

Page Insights is a free service from Facebook, which allows you to view your page performance as a whole. Displaying information in a graph, it offers a range of metric data, from net increase in likes to a comparison of organic vs paid reach and visits to your page and posts.

Pros

- Offers a host of different metrics, including demographic information
- Easy to use graphs which can be lifted directly to create reports and presentations
- Helps you understand the people who make up your audience

Cons

- Fairly static – you can only define your parameters and data ranges on certain metrics
- There can be some discrepancies between likes, comments and shares displayed and actual engagement

Facebook Adverts Manager

Facebook Adverts Manager gives you the ability to track an individual advert or campaign's performance and monitor your spend and budget. The interface shows frequency, reach, impressions, unique clicks, click-through rate and action taken as a result of your adverts.

Pros

- Constantly evolving with new features
- Simplifies keeping track of your ad spend
- Allows you to assign up to six image variants to each advert, making it easy to a/b test your advert performance
- Specific filtering methods available that allow you to pinpoint key demographics, interests and buying behaviour

Cons

- Not as robust as Google Analytics
- Can show discrepancies between clicks (paid) and actual sessions on the website
- Cost per click is increasing

LinkedIn: Who's viewed your profile and how you rank for profile views

As a standard feature, LinkedIn now includes details about who has viewed your profile and where you rank within your network for profile views. This tool gives a very basic overview of how you're performing on the platform.

Pros

- Incentivises you to improve your profile, if your profile views are low
- Displays who is viewing your profile allowing you to analyse if you're visible to the right people from the right industries
- Allows you to analyse those who are top within your network to see how you compare
- Suggests ways to enhance your profile to improve page views and rank

Cons

- A LinkedIn Premium account is needed for more detailed insights
- No breakdown of content performance is available

LinkedIn: Campaign Manager

When using LinkedIn for business, you may consider using the sponsored updates feature to boost your content. Their advert analytics platform gives insight into your engaged audience, impressions and clicks and allows you to monitor and control your budget.

Pros

- Specific targeting methods are available
- The lead connection function allows you to follow up on those who click your ad
- View your impressions, clicks, leads and cost per click from your ads table
- View the industries and job roles of your campaign's engaged audience
- Metric data is available in graph format

Cons

- Difficult to edit campaigns from the home dashboard
- No search feature for finding your campaigns or adverts
- Lack of bulk editing features
- No conversion tracking

Pinterest

Pinterest Analytics

For those with a Pinterest for Business account, you can get access to Pinterest's analytics feature. Use Pinterest Analytics to review and track the performance of your pins regularly.

Pros

- See your most viewed and most pinned content
- Access your audience's demographic information and interests
- View what devices people use when pinning
- Analyse where your referral traffic is coming from

Cons

- Only available to Pinterest for Business users
- Only shows information about your own content (as opposed to other people's content that you've re-pinned)
- Only shows data from the date you verified your website

Instagram

At the time of writing, Instagram have only just rolled out their advertising service and at present it is not widely available to all users. Although in its infancy, as a part of this roll-out they have incorporated some new tools on the platform, which include account insights and ad insights, both of which aim to help brands assess their performance.

Advertisers using the service have access to real time data, including insights into how their target audience is responding to their content, in a similar style to Facebook Insights.

Another interesting development is the ad staging tool, which allows marketers to create, edit and collaborate with others on their paid adverts, before they go live.

YouTube Analytics

If you're publishing content to YouTube, you need to make sure you're analysing the performance of your videos. One of the most important factors to consider is your total view count, but there are more important metrics to consider – all of which are available using YouTube's Analytics platform.

Pros

- Discover the source of traffic to your video
- Provides a geographical and demographic breakdown of your audience
- Understand audience retention
- Gives an overview of subscribers
- Allows you to understand how often your video is shared socially
- Available to all users

Cons

- Video display is not customisable
- To access full range of analytics you must become a YouTube Partner (meaning you must display ads)
- The platform is not as simple to use as other services, such as Wistia

**IF YOU REMEMBER
ONE LAST THING**

**It's very easy to become obsessed with the numbers
when it comes to digital marketing.**

If you're not clear what numbers will deliver on your business objectives,
you're wasting valuable time and falling into a very densely populated trap.

Make sure you have full visibility of your net results and a clear breakdown of
where you're investing your time and how it's impacting your business goals
Keep it as simple as possible and don't compromise with technology.

Market your business in the modern age and have a dashboard that helps
you drive towards your destination with confidence and clarity. Continually
review your goals and results, and modify and evolve your strategy based on
what is going well and what isn't.

It's that easy.

Recommended reading & resources

BOOKS

Inbound Marketing
Brian Halligan and Dharmesh Shah

This book from the founders of HubSpot is a comprehensive guide to increasing online visibility and engagement. Written by top marketing and start-up bloggers, the book contains the latest information about customer behaviour and preferred digital experiences. From the latest insights on lead nurturing and visual marketing to advice on producing remarkable content by building tools, readers will gain the information they need to transform their marketing online.

Watertight Marketing: Delivering Long-Term Sales Results
Bryony Thomas

A straightforward, straight talking book, Watertight Marketing takes an in-depth look at how inbound marketing disciplines can directly influence the fundamentals of any business.

Socialize to Monetize
Gabriela Taylor

Socialize to Monetize takes you through 25 of the major social networking sites, from setting them up through to how they can be effectively leveraged to generate maximum return.

ONLINE TOOLS

Sprout Social

A comprehensive social media management tool, Sprout Social features a bespoke analysis and reporting function. You can report across multiple platforms or produce in-depth reports on individual channels, assessing the reach and resonance of your messages.
sproutsocial.com

Crazy Egg

Crazy Egg provides a heat map visualisation of where in your content people are clicking and what parts of your page are viewed most often. This is particularly useful for assessing landing pages, allowing you to customise your content around the places that are being interacted with.
crazyegg.com

HubSpot

Having coined the term 'Inbound Marketing', HubSpot have created one of the best tools in the business to enhance your inbound marketing strategy. Helping you to identify and maximise your buyer personas, attract visitors, convert leads and close customers, it pretty much does it all.
hubspot.com

Google Analytics

Google Analytics is an essential tool in understanding your website traffic sources, ecommerce goals, search terms and audience demographics.

google.com/analytics

Dash This

Dash This makes your reporting tasks simple, and pulls information from a range of sources. Allowing you to create weekly, monthly, quarterly and annual reports and providing an instant snapshot of your performance, Dash This is a great tool to add to your armoury.

dashthis.com

Radian 6

Track your conversions across different social platforms and manage multiple social media accounts and campaigns from one dashboard. Allowing you to monitor social mentions across the web, you can gain valuable insights into the conversations your target personas are having online and engage with them on a personal level.

goo.gl/edEeAU

Meltwater Buzz

Monitor your social media engagement and analytics through the Meltwater Buzz intelligence platform. Allowing you to develop stronger brand relationships and gain a fuller understanding of your social marketing campaigns, this tool helps you recognise your social media ROI and act on it.

meltwater.com

SourceHub

SourceHub, from Social Talent is a fantastic tool which allows you to generate Boolean search strings for recruiting online. Significantly cutting the time and effort involved in recruiting using LinkedIn, SourceHub can help you find the right candidates quickly and simply.

source.socialtalent.co

Marketing automation download

Download our guide to marketing automation at the link below and start streamlining the way you manage your inbound marketing.

ph-creative.com/Chapter8Resources

Key takeaways for chapter 8

Now your strategy is in place and your tactics planned and considered, it's time to think about measuring your success. Check off each of the below points as you complete them.

☐ Invest in one clear and concise tool to keep track of your marketing activity

☐ Ask your customer's opinions on your business

☐ Work out your conversion rate (and how to improve it)

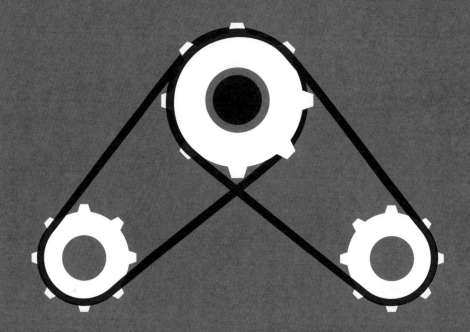

And finally...

So there you have it. The end of our whistle stop tour of the tools and resources you need to get started to build your own robust and deliverable inbound marketing strategy.

The great thing about inbound marketing is that it's almost a living, breathing thing itself. Constantly evolving with tastes and trends, there is very rarely a dull moment. That's because it's about people and it's about conversations.

There will never be a definitive formula for your inbound marketing and, for us, that's the beauty of it. It will always be about creativity and vision. However, what you'll find here is a tried and tested recipe for success that will help you to create contagious content so powerful it gives your audience goosebumps.

All too often, when you're out on the frontline, it's easy to forget the human element behind marketing – we become too bogged down in numbers and tactics without thinking about crafting emotion and effective storytelling into the message.

Now that times are changing, you've got to get creative and reactive. Having your finger on the pulse of digital trends will help you to remain consistently aware of your customers' needs and desires. CEOs of companies including Blockbuster, Woolworths and HMV would all quietly testify to the importance of moving with the times and embracing change.

So the question is, are you ready to embrace inbound marketing? Are you ready to change your mindset and fundamentally shift the way you think about being successful in the digital space?

From CEOs to bedroom marketers, this book will hopefully have reignited your passion for marketing, highlighted the importance of emotion, storytelling, research and analysis and got you fired up and ready to tackle your next challenge.

By following the principles and philosophy laid out in this book you can start to measure the results of your marketing more effectively and demonstrate the return on investment of your activities – the quickest way to increase your marketing budget and earn the reputation you're looking for.

Get ready to harness new technology and drive your marketing forward with confidence – cutting out the guess work and achieving the traction and results that you need to survive and prosper. You should be starting to understand that through investing in content that resonates with your audience you can create real, rewarding engagement.

We've walked you through everything from defining your brand and understanding your audience to telling a story and measuring your success. We've supplied you with all the components, tools and tips you need to create an inbound strategy that starts generating real results. All that's left is for you to get started.

Don't wait for the marketplace and your customers to demand you work in this way, get out there first and make an impact on your business, before the rest of the world catches up. It's about learning how to dominate your space with a voice that resonates across a transmedia landscape. When that message lands, it's magnetic, it's contagious and you're Getting Goosebumps.

Glossary

AD SPEND – the amount of money spent on both on and offline advertising and promotions

ADVOCACY – public support for, or recommendation of, a particular cause or policy

AUDIENCE SEGMENTATION – the process of dividing people into homogeneous subgroups based upon defined criteria such as product usage, demographics, psychographics, communication behaviours and media use

AUTHORITATIVE CONTENT – content which establishes the author as a source of authority and trust

BLOG – a regularly updated website or web page, written in an informal or conversational style

BRAND VALUES – the core values that define your company's strengths and differentiate you from your competitors

BUYING PROCESS – the series of steps that a consumer will take to make a purchasing decision

BUZZWORDS – a word or phrase that is fashionable at a particular time or in a particular context

CALL TO ACTION – an instruction to the audience to provoke an immediate response, usually using an imperative verb such as 'call now', 'find out more' or 'visit a store today'

CAMPAIGN – an organised course of action to promote a product or service

'DELIGHT' CONTENT – keywords, language and content that is designed to add value to existing customers or known prospects in order to retain them, add value and provide ongoing opportunity whatever that might be

DEMOGRAPHIC – the quantifiable statistics of a given group or population

'DO' CONTENT – keywords, language and content that are designed to convince a relatively qualified audience to take some form of action. This might not be moving in for an immediate sale, but it could be a download, a request for a call, or more information

EGO-JACKING – the process of positively recommending an influencer within your content, with the aim of provoking them to share your content

ENGAGEMENT – the interaction between customers or with a company or a brand

INFLUENCERS – individuals who have the power to affect purchase decisions of others because of their (real or perceived) authority, knowledge, position, or relationship

INFOGRAPHIC – a visual representation of information or data

KEYWORDS – terms which relate directly to your product/service and are likely to be searched for by your audience

LANDING PAGE – a web page which serves as the entry point for a website or a particular section of a website

LONG TAIL KEYWORDS – keyword phrases that consist of between two and five words, usually used when searching for a specific item

NEWS-JACKING – the practice of capitalising on the popularity of a news story to amplify your sales and marketing success

OUTREACH – creatively reaching out to brands/businesses/clients with a creative solution or offer

PATHOS – a direct appeal to the emotions of your audience

RANKING – your position on a search engine results page, in response to keywords, content and links included within your site

RESPONSIVE – a web design approach aimed at crafting sites to provide an optimal viewing experience across a wide range of devices

SALES FUNNEL – a visual representation of where your buyers are on their purchasing journey

SCHEMA – additional tagging of content, within the code of a page that provides search engines with additional context surrounding the content on your website

'SEE' CONTENT – keywords, language and content that is designed to attract new, uninitiated 'strangers' at the start of the buying journey

SEEDING – finding and approaching influential web and blog editors who will find your content interesting and engaging, so much so that they will want to share it with their visitors

SEO – the process of affecting the visibility of a website or a web page in a search engine's natural or un-paid (organic) search results

SOCIAL AMPLIFICATION – the concept of taking a positive action – a purchase, a light-touch interaction or full-on review – saving it and then sharing it far and wide, through organic or paid methods

SOCIAL PROOF – also known as informational social influence, social proof is a psychological phenomenon where people assume the actions of others in an attempt to reflect correct behaviour for a given situation

SOCIAL SPACE – a physical or virtual space such as a social centre, online social network, or other gathering place where people gather and interact

SPLIT TESTING – also referred to as A/B testing or multivariate testing, is a method of conducting controlled, randomised experiments with the goal of improving a website metric, such as clicks, form completions, or purchases

STRATEGY – a plan of action designed to achieve a long-term or overall aim

'THINK' CONTENT – keywords, language and content that is designed to provide material surrounding your brand and the specific initial needs of your audience. This content adds value to the process by connecting the benefits of your offer with the intrinsic needs of the audience

WEBINAR – a seminar conducted over the internet

WORD OF MOUTH MARKETING – the passing of information between a non-commercial communicator (i.e. someone who is not rewarded) and a receiver, concerning a brand, product, or service

How **Ph.Creative** can help you

Established for over 10 years, everything we do is focused on delivering remarkable results. Our insight, creativity and expertise will help you to effectively tell your brand story and engage with your audience, whilst consistently hitting your top line objectives.

Whether you need responsive web design or a remarkable inbound marketing campaign, we'll make sure your brand's voice stands out from the crowd.

WHAT WE DO

- Web design and development
- E-commerce
- Inbound marketing
- Social media
- CRO
- SEO
- PPC
- UI and UX design
- Strategy
- Video production
- Social advertising

OUR SERVICES

- Consultancy
- Inbound marketing retainer
- Audience/persona mapping workshop
- Audience/persona mapping validation
- Website and social media audit
- Strategic planning workshops
- Creative ideas workshops
- Website development
- Marketing automation planning & design
- Employer brand / EVP strategy, tactics and management
- Talent attraction strategy, tactics and management
- Employee engagement
- Candidate experience design
- Careers technology design and development

Staying in touch

More than anything else, we'd love to receive feedback, stories or anecdotes of how this book has helped you progress your business in some way.

We'd also love to answer any further questions you may have especially if we've sparked a new passion or interest with our ideas. With this in mind here's a few ways you can engage with us and stay in touch.

Or, of course, you could visit our website at **ph-creative.com**

You can also book us for a conference keynote presentation. We're not just smart cookies, we're also a devilishly handsome, witty and charismatic bunch of people (especially Bryan, who had final edit on this page!). We can be booked directly via our website or via a number of speaker agencies.

Email us: **hello@ph-creative.com**

Bryan:
Twitter - **@Bryan_phc**
LinkedIn - **uk.linkedin.com/in/bryanadams1**
Instagram - **@Bryan_phc**
Pinterest - **pinterest.com/bryanphc**

Dave:
Twitter - **@googledave**
LinkedIn - **uk.linkedin.com/in/googledave**
Google+ - **plus.google.com/+DaveHazlehurst**

Ph.Creative

Twitter
@phcreative

LinkedIn
uk.linkedin.com/company/ph.creative

Google+
plus.google.com/+PhcreativeLiverpool

Facebook
facebook.com/Ph.Headquarters

Instagram
@ph.creative/

Pinterest
pinterest.com/phcreative/

Vimeo
vimeo.com/phcreativevideo

YouTube
youtube.com/user/PhCreativeVideo